"This is a book for writers and readers, for those uncertain and certain of God. Woiwode's examination of literature is so masterful that one can't help but weigh his prose hand in hand with the art he admires, and I will not be surprised if you should find his sentences richer. I've been a student of Woiwode's work for thirty years and am not yet done—this stunning collection of thought and prose has made me think and dream as I haven't in years."

G. W. Hawkes, Professor of English, Co-Director Creative Writing, Lycoming College

"Larry Woiwode is an American original. His thoughts and words serve up a rich intellectual feast, causing the reader at times to raise an eyebrow in uncertainty, at times to smile with pleasure, and always to feel rewarded."

Philip Yancey, best-selling author, *What's So Amazing About Grace?*

"Woiwode's collection of essays showcases the finest features of this great American writer: an authentic voice and point of view. Now lambent, now strident, the essays, which range from guns, Gardner, and God, to Updike and Shakespeare, evince Woiwode's formidable critical clarity and intellectual acuity."

Ellen Lansky, author, *Golden Jeep*

"Living up to the inventiveness of the book's title, these essays are fireside chats with a well-known author on a range of subjects—literary criticism to cultural critique. The result is a valuable blend of information and assessment of culture and authors ranging from modern writers like John Updike and Reynolds Price to William Shakespeare (the subject of the culminating essay in the book, a small classic)."

Leland Ryken, Professor of English, Wheaton College

"A pilgrimage of power and delight: beginning with an intellect as brilliant and widespread as a prairie nighttime sky, to a spirit as revelatory and pure as a child observing that same prairie's flowers. To read Woiwode is to learn, to know, to understand, and to be amazed by workmanship."

John L. Moore, author, *The Breaking of Ezra Riley*, *Take the Reins*, and *Bitter Roots*

"*Words Made Fresh* is an urgently important chance to understand the beliefs of a great American writer."

Thomas McGuane, author, *Ninety-Two in the Shade*

"Larry Woiwode is as gifted an essayist as he is a novelist, bringing something rare in today's literary culture—intellectual engagement grounded in spirituality—to each offering in *Words Made Fresh*. As with his outstanding fiction, these reflections on literature and culture are not only refreshing but deeply rewarding."

> **Charles Johnson,** award-winning author, *Middle Passage*;
> Professor Emeritus of English, University of Washington

"An ideal essay collection is one that makes me feel as if I should sit down in a book-lined den and read at leisure. That's what Woiwode accomplishes here as he breaks the bread and pours the wine of favorite books, authors, and challenging ideas, all of it informed by a deep respect for humans and the God who created them. Reading through this collection I couldn't help but delight in the quality of the mind behind the vigorous prose and the unfolding transformation of my understanding."

> **Albert Haley,** writer in residence, Abilene Christian University;
> author, *Home Ground: Stories of Two Families and the Land*

"A kaleidoscopic and fascinating commentary on literary things, much of it over my head, but now and again touching my heart."

> **G. I. Williamson,** retired minister, Orthodox Presbyterian Church;
> author, *Westminster Confession of Faith: For Study Classes*

"Mark me among those who admire just about everything Larry Woiwode touches with his pen. Few American writers achieve the elegance he does with nearly every sentence. Whether story or essay, the music in his prose is a joy, a wonder, a gift of grace. *Words Made Fresh* is as refreshing as it is insightful, and Woiwode's critiques of Berry, Gardner, Updike, and others are as thoughtful and precise as we would expect from a writer so greatly gifted."

> **Jim Schaap,** Professor of English, Dordt College

"Great writing is greatest when its weft and warp are inseparable, when what is being said weaves so tightly into how it is said that new meanings are brought forth, and whole tapestried landscapes are suddenly apprehended. *Words Made Fresh*, in its omnivorous density, in its evenhandedness that reveals a lapidary perspective, in its moral engagement and in its fuerte of feeling, is great writing at its greatest."

> **Lynn Stegner,** Lecturer in Continuing Studies, Stanford University;
> author, *Because a Fire Was in My Head*

"This absorbing collection of essays presents Woiwode at his most insightful and most provocative. Woiwode provides astute analysis and sensitive observations, linking personal narrative with commentary on the Word and its connections with and disconnections from contemporary culture. He is not only one of our finest novelists, Woiwode also offers a strong Christian aesthetic and a cultural savvy that is penetrating and wise."

Jill Peláez Baumgaertner, Dean of Humanities and Theological Studies, Wheaton College

"Larry Woiwode's prose is so piercing and precise, so concrete and muscular, that I would read his reflections on the price of potatoes. In an era when words have become weapons or commodities, Woiwode reminds us that they can still become flesh and blood, full of grace and truth."

Gregory Wolfe, publisher, editor, *Image*; writer in residence, director of MFA in Creative Writing program, Seattle Pacific University

"Reading these essays brought back a wonderful year spent in Finland, much of it with *Mickelsson's Ghosts*, a book I loved but hadn't had a way to think about until now. I felt the same returning to Updike, someone I've taught, but not with this sort of precision and sympathy and wariness. This is what writing looks like from the inside. Woiwode and the writers he focuses on feel God's presence like a steady pressure, all but taking the breath away. They show us what it's like to respond to that pressure—in time, in a body, here on this earth."

Thomas Gardner, Professor of English, Virginia Tech; author, *A Door Ajar: Contemporary Writers and Emily Dickinson*

"With each of his books, Woiwode offers tantalizing and challenging insight into creation, fall, and redemption. As always, we read Woiwode's *Words Made Fresh* because we need to and because we find that easily forgotten blessing: delight!"

Rick Watson, Professor of English, Minot State University; North Dakota Associate Poet Laureate

"A magnificent crunch of words to their essence. Woiwode at his best. A true great American writer."

Timothy Strong, bookseller, The Birchbark Bookshop, Potsdam, New York

WORDS MADE FRESH

WORDS MADE FRESH

Essays on Literature and Culture

LARRY WOIWODE

CROSSWAY
WHEATON, ILLINOIS

Words Made Fresh: Essays on Literature and Culture

Copyright © 2011 by Larry Woiwode

Published by Crossway
    1300 Crescent Street
    Wheaton, Illinois 60187

Cover design: Studio Gearbox

Cover photos: iStock, Photos.com, Veer

First printing 2011

Printed in the United States of America

ISBN: 978-1-4335-2740-1

PDF ISBN: 978-1-4335-2741-8

Mobipocket ISBN: 978-1-4335-2742-5

ePub ISBN: 978-1-4335-2743-2

Library of Congress Cataloging-in-Publication Data
Woiwode, Larry.
 Words made fresh : essays on literature and culture / Larry Woiwode
  p. cm.
 ISBN 978-1-4335-2740-1 (hc)
 I. Title.
PS3573.O4W67   2011
814'.54—dc222010053227

Crossway is a publishing ministry of Good News Publishers.

TS		20	19	18	17	16	15	14	13	12	11
14	13	12	11	10	9	8	7	6	5	4	3	2	1

To
CAROLE
December 10, 2009

CONTENTS

INTRODUCTION

My title is meant to echo the incarnation, because it was with the incarnation that writers outside the scope of the Hebrew or Greek texts began to understand how a metaphor of words could contain the lineaments and inner workings of a human being. The Hebrew Bible supplied the earliest clues, since it didn't merely list a set of rules to regulate social behavior, as for instance the Code of Hammurabi did, but was an ordering of stories that revealed not only heroic actions of certain individuals but also a bleak black side to others, along with glimpses into character: Moses's pretense that he couldn't speak in public (after being reared in the court of Egypt), Saul's cries for calming music, David's gold hair like the glow of his personality, Jephthah making good his rash vow.

The title also issues an assurance that the following essays, which appeared in a variety of venues over the years, have been revised or reworked and otherwise brought up to date, so that the words forming the phrases and sentences and thoughts in the paragraphs ahead have, indeed, been refashioned, made fresh.

Guns & Peace

On an American Icon

Once in the worst of a Wisconsin winter I shot a deer, my only one, while my wife and daughter watched. The deer had been hit by a delivery truck along a county road a few miles from where we lived, and one of its rear legs was torn off at the hock. A shattered shin and hoof lay steaming in the red-beaded ice on the road. The driver of the truck and I stood and watched as the deer tried to leap a fence, kicked a while at the top wire its stub was entangled in, flailing the area with fresh ropes of blood, and then went hobbling across a pasture toward a wooded hill. Snow-covered cows followed it with a curious awe.

"Do you have a rifle with you?" the driver asked.

"Not on me, no. At home."

He glanced toward the deer once more, and then got in his truck and drove off.

I went back to our vehicle, where my wife and daughter were waiting, pale and withdrawn, and told them what I intended to do, and, on the drive back, suggested they'd better stay at home.

No, they wanted to be with me, they said; they wanted to watch. Our daughter was going on four that winter. I got my rifle, a .22, a foolishly puny weapon to use on a deer but the only one I had, and we drove back. I saw that the deer was lying in low brush near the base of the wooded hill—no need to trail its blatant spoor. When I got a hundred yards off, marveling how the deer could make it so far in its condition through snow that rose over my boot tops, it tried to push itself up with its front legs, and then collapsed. I aimed at the center of its skull, thinking, This will be the quickest, and heard the bullet ricochet off and go singing through the trees.

The deer was on its feet, shaking its head as though stung, and I fired at the same spot, quickly, and apparently missed. It was moving in its fastest hobble up the hill, broadside to me, and I took time to sight a heart shot. Before the report even registered in my mind, the deer was down in an explosion of snow and lay struggling, spouting blood from its stump and a chest wound. I was shaking by now. Deer are color blind, science says, which is why hunters wear orange, and as I went toward the deer to deliver the coup de grace, I realized it was seeing me in black and white, and then its eye homed in on me, and I understood I was its vision of approaching death. And with that I seemed to enter its realm, through its eye, and saw myself and the countryside in shades of white and gray.

But I see the deer in color, I thought.

A few yards away I aimed at its head once more and heard the crack of a shot, the next-to-last round left in the magazine—all the cartridges I'd brought in my hurry. The deer's head came up, and I could see its eye clearly now, dark, placid, filled with an appeal, it seemed, and I felt the surge of black and white overtake me again. The second shot, or one of them, had pierced its neck. Its gray-blue tongue hung out the side of its jaw; urine was trickling from below its tail. A doe. I pointed the end of the barrel close to its forehead, conscious of my wife's and daughter's eyes on me from behind and, as I fired off the fatal shot, felt drawn by them into my multi-colored, many-faceted world again.

I don't remember the first gun I fired, the heritage is so ingrained in me, but I know I've used a variety of weapons to kill birds, reptiles, amphibians, plant life, insects (bees and butterflies with a shotgun), fish that came too close to shore, small mammals, that deer—never a human being, I'm quick to interject, although the accumulated carnage I've put away with bullets since boyhood is probably enough to add up to a couple of cows, not counting the deer. I've fired at targets, both living and inert, using an elderly ten-gauge with double hammers that left a welt on my shoulder that stayed a week; also a Mauser, a twelve-gauge sawed-off shotgun, an SKS, an M-16, a .222, a 30.06 and a 30.30, a dozen variations on the .22—pump, bolt action, lever action, special scopes and sights and stocks—a .410 over-and-under, a zip gun that blew up and left a piece of shrapnel imbedded in my left arm, an Italian carbine, a .22 revolver, a Luger, a .45, and, among others, a fancily engraved, single-trigger, double-barrel, twenty-gauge at snowballs thrown from behind my back over a bluff. And on that same bluff on a New Year's Day in the seventies, after some wine and prodding, I found myself at the jittering ring of stutters from a paratrooper's machine gun with a collapsible, geo-metrically reinforced metal stock, and watched its spouting tracers go off across the night toward the already-set sun, realizing this was probably the hundredth weapon I'd had performing in my hands, and this, the most potentially destructive, was the newest one.

I grew up in North Dakota, at the edge of the West, during the turbulence and then the aftermath of World War II, which America won in such an outright way there was a sense of vindication about the country's long-standing love of guns—not to say pride in them, too. "Bang! Bang! You're dead," returns to me from that time without the least speck of friction against conscience or time. When my friends and I weren't playing War, or Cowboys and Indians, or Cops and Robbers, we were reading war comics (from which you could order for ninety-nine cents miniature cardboard chests of plastic weaponry and soldiers) or Westerns, or listening to *The Lone Ranger*, who fired off five shots before his program even began, or *Richard Diamond, Private Detective* or *Dragnet* and other radio dramas that generally glorified guns—and the more powerful, the better.

My fantasies, when I was frustrated or irate, were rife with firearms of the most lethal sort, flying shot or rounds of shattering ammunition, leaving the enemy bodies blown away in bloody tableaux. The imagery was present whenever I picked up a comic book or went to the movies or, later, turned on the TV—all of them flashy, one-dimensional forms of communication that didn't convey the substantiality of real life, much less the ethical concerns each decision is fraught with, but strobed so far into a realm of primitive energy I could never wholly shake them as a young person. The images were reinforced often, in such an offhand manner, they seemed everyday events in the wider arena of existence. In that arena, adults were the arbiters, and it was adults who had the guns. They were so potentially destructive, no young person would imagine carrying one to school.

I've owned three firearms in my life until recently. Two of them I took back to the shops within a week after I'd bought them, subdued by a sense of trying to reach out in an archaic way, and the limits to maturity and imagination that this implied, plus the bother to my daughter of their explosive noise. And the third, the .22 I carried on my trek to the deer, after trembling over it a few years and once using it to shoot holes in the floor between my feet to enact a mock suicide, I gave away. To my younger brother.

He was initiated into the buck-fever fraternity in the forest of northern Wisconsin when he was an adolescent by a seasoned local who said, "If you see anything out there tomorrow, boy, shoot it. You can check out later what it was. Nobody gives a diddly up here." Thus the orange, to protect hunters from other hunters. On a hunting trip a few years later, an acquaintance from the village my brother lived in then, a lawyer, was shot in the head with a deer rifle but somehow survived, and even went back to practicing law. It was believed to be an accident at first, with all the bullets embroidering the air that day; and then rumor had it that another member of a party hunting on adjoining land, an old friend of the lawyer's, had found out a week before that the lawyer had been having his wife. The two men were polite enough to each other in the village after that, my brother said, but not such good friends, of course—just-balanced, justice-balanced males.

For weeks after I shot the crippled doe, every time we drove past the field, our daughter would say, "Here's where Daddy shooted the deer." In exactly that manner, in the tone and detachment of a tourist guide. And I would glance into the rearview mirror and see her in her car seat, studying the hill with troubled, sympathetic eyes.

One day I pulled over and stopped. "Does it bother you so much that I shot it?" I asked. There was no answer, and then I noticed she was nodding her head, her large eyes fixed on the hill.

"If I wouldn't have, it could have suffered a long time. You saw how badly hurt it was. It couldn't have lived that way. I didn't like doing it, either, but in the long run it was best for the deer. When I reported it to the game warden, he even thanked me and said, 'Leave it for the foxes and crows.' They have to eat, too, you know, and maybe the deer made the winter easier for them."

And I thought, Oh, what a self-justifying hypocrite you are! Why didn't you leave her at home? Or go to the farmer whose land the deer was on—which would have been quicker than going home for the .22 and back—a person who would have had a deer rifle, or at least a shotgun with rifled slugs, and could have put the deer away with dispatch—might have salvaged even the hide and venison? And who could say it wouldn't have lived, the way some animals do after tearing or chewing off a foot caught in a trap?

Who was I to presume it wouldn't have preferred to die a slow death in the woods, looking out over the pasture, as the crimson stain widening in the snow dimmed its colorless world until all went black? Why not admit I was an American of a certain backcountry kind and, like many of my mold, had used an arsenal of firearms, and was as excited about putting a deer away, at last, as I was troubled by its suffering? Then again, given my daughter's intuitiveness and the person I am, perhaps she sensed that.

I once choked a chicken to death. It was my only one-on-one, barefaced, not to say bare-handed, confrontation with death and the killer in me. It took place on my grandparents' farm. I couldn't have been more than nine, and no firearms were present. I was on my knees, the chicken fluttering its outstretched wings, unable to release any protest past my grip above its swollen crop, beak gaping, translucent eyelids sliding up and down. An old molting specimen, probably past laying age. Malthus. Eugenics. Better for it. Any excuse. If it was laying, or might again, a worse loss than a capon or cock. My grandfather, who was widely traveled and worldly wise, in his seventies then, and had started using a cane due to an injury, came tapping at that moment around the corner of the chicken coop and saw what I was doing and blanched at the sight, gagged, I believe, then did a quick turnaround on his cane and never again, hours later or for the rest of his life, mentioned the incident to me. My mother, his daughter, had died the winter before, and he may have known I needed to see the passage from life to death (so I say now) take place in my hands. In some sense, since he kept his silence, he seemed to understand; but whenever I'm invaded by the incident, the point of it seems his horrified look and his turning away from me.

My wife once said she felt I wanted to kill her, a common enough apprehension among married couples, I'm sure, and not restricted to either sex (I know there were times when she wanted to kill me), but perhaps with experience infusing the feeling it became too much to endure. I now live in New York City, alone, where the calendar and clock keep me tending toward my suitcase for yet another trip, and she and my daughter live in Chicago. The city has changed in the years since the three of us lived here. There are more frivolous wares—silk kerchiefs, necklaces and rings, roach clips, rolling papers, a display of Florida coral across a convertible top, books of every kind—being sold on the streets than anybody can remember. Street people are saying that soon it will be like the thirties again, with all of us on the streets selling our apples, or whatever, engaged in a tacit and comradely kind of gangsterism to survive. Outside my window, a spindly deciduous species has a sign strung on supporting posts on either side of it, in careful hand lettering, that reads, "THIS TREE GIVES OXYGEN, GIVE IT LOVE."

There are more dogs in the streets and parks and more canine offal sending up its open-ended odor; at least half the population has given up smoking, at last, for good, they say, and many actually have. There is an amazed feeling, present most everywhere, of being in the midst of a slowly forging reciprocity, along with an air of bravura in maintaining one's best face, with a few changes of costuming to reflect that, no matter what might yet evolve—a unisex barbershop or boutique on nearly every other block.

Sometimes I think this is where I belong. Then somebody is gunned down in a neighborhood hangout I used to visit, and the next day a mafia boss is assassinated, reportedly by members of his own mob, in a place farther uptown. Or this is where I feel most at home, I equivocate, and see myself in a Stetson traveling down a crosstown street at a fast-paced and pigeon-toed hurry toward the setting sun (setting here, but not over my wife and daughter yet), my eyes cast down and hands deep in my empty Levi pockets, a suspect, closet comedy act occasionally whistled at by guys.

I can't refute my heritage, but I doubt that I'll use a firearm again, certainly not in the city, and, if outside it, only in the direst emergency. Which I say to protect my flanks. The bloody, gun-filled fantasies seldom return, now that layers of realistic literature crowd my head, and when they do they're reversed. I'm the one being shot, or shot full of holes, as if the primitive portion of my imagination keeps insisting this is what I deserve.

*   *   *

AFTERWORD: What I deserved led me to understand the full and free payment of my just deserts. The essay was written and set in the midseventies, although portions of it, including auras of the city, are as relevant in 2010. My wife and I reunited and reared our daughter and two more daughters, plus a son, on a ranch in western North Dakota. In this incarnation I own firearms, mainly for predators, especially rabid ones, and I do not cling to them as I cling to the faith that reunited my wife and me and caused our internal lives and the lives of our children to blossom and prosper in peace.

Homeplace, Heaven
or Hell?

On the Order of Existence

When a writer crosses the line of impropriety and talks about the act
of writing itself, he or she'd better speak about it from the inside, as
a person in a suit of armor might describe an itch starting to crawl
up an arm, not as a scholar focusing on the makeup of a medieval
gorget of mail. The itch in this instance is the relevance of place, or
locale, to contemporary fiction.

The French novelist Georges Bernanos says about his native
Provence in *Essais et écrits de combat I*, after being absent from it
for thirty years,

> Whether here or there, why should I be nostalgic about what
> actually belongs to me, is mine, and which I cannot betray? Why
> should I invoke the black puddles of the beaten-down path, or the
> hedge resounding under the melancholy beating of the rain since
> I am myself both the hedge and the black puddles?[1]

Here is a heartfelt response to homeplace, in which details of
a particular place become one with the writer. Some critics might
view Bernanos's response as regional. When canonmeisters label a

writer "regional," they suggest that the writer isn't in quite the same league as the big boys, equating regionalism with parochialism—an attitude that honors certain areas of the United States (or the world, for that matter) as right and proper, preferable to others—while the rest is regional. Every traveler knows that the vast tracts of continent from New Jersey to California contain varieties of typography, though some travelers might feel a sort of homogenous blandness begins in Ohio and isn't quite healed until the Pacific Coast. The area is called the Midwest, although it contains areas of the East and Northwest and West.

In our anxious modern tendency to categorize—a reflex that suggests fear and has its apotheosis in computer circuits, as if fear dictates even the patterns of organization in the machines we invent to think for us—we seem to have forgotten the unpronounceable county in Mississippi, whose creator said it was the size of a postage stamp, or the locale of the odyssey of our latter-day Ulysses, Dublin, or the best-selling prophet who never strayed far from his birthplace, Bethlehem.

Let me say, then, that the properties of a particular place are important, yes, but that human beings are more important than locale. And the inner state of a character is of far greater importance than any external estate containing him or her, no matter how extraordinary its geophysical distinctions. Of even greater import is the character's need to relate events that have had an emotional effect on his or her character to a friend or neighbor, the auditor of fiction.

Those elements make up what is known as narrative, and they can be transferred to any landscape on the planet, or to any vehicle in orbit around it. In one of the most limited poems, William Blake gives voice to a clod of clay and a pebble in a brook.[2] It's difficult to narrow your vision more than that, though Theodore Roethke does in his greenhouse poems.[3] In the "The Clod and the Pebble," Blake dramatizes self-centered and selfless love, and by implication suggests that selfless love renders living in the world bearable, if it isn't the foundation on which redeeming life in the world is built. It might help to have a Christian perspective to arrive at this last, larger inference (the clay as God-man trod down) but the poem is one that anybody from any culture at any given period can pick up and resonate to, as with Bernanos. Both speak to an unequivocal nature in every human being.

So it's time to shed one obvious misapprehension about writing—that the physical locus of a piece of fiction limits the way in which meaning may widen from it, as rings of water widen around a cattail that a blackbird abandons. I can indeed reverse the premise and say that to the degree writing is true to indigenous detail, to that degree it resonates with wider meaning—or universality, as some might say. Think of the young man from rural Stratford who never forgot the local flora or any Bottom or Dogberry or resident of Arden, or the poetic, power-stricken Richards who aspired to be kings of one kind or another.

The writing I refer to is of the compressed specificity found in poetry and fiction. Such writing has its ear to the pulse of people, who are at the heart of writing, whatever form it takes, and by conveying the feelings of a particular person, that writing connects with humankind. An unfolding story begins to take its course, and story examines the passage of light or darkness in each individual, common to the flaws and scars all of us bear. Descriptive prose examines only appearances, as if the suit of armor or clothes on one's back is the person—prose that goes out of fashion as quickly as clothes themselves. That sort of writing could be called sociographic news and is not the writing I want to linger over.

Writers such as Wendell Berry, who settle in their native home place, are seen as "going back to the land." Part of the motivation behind Berry and writers akin to him has roots in the Agrarian movement, and for others it may be romantic modishness rising from the sixties—ecology, back to nature, the natural world, and the like. Writers who settle outside city boundaries are often termed regional or terminal regionalists. A writer who limits the scope of a work to a known environment, and then narrows the focus within that environment, is liable to receive that title nowadays, rather than the one that has served for centuries: a poet.

Universality is compounded of specifics, or we have no referent to relate to, and a writer is no more local than clods or stones or trees or animals or flowing water (with variations in types or shapes or species) or individual vision, or imagination itself, is local. A more useful division might be between writers who wish to reside in and refer to nature, a universal phenomenon, or to live in the academy or the city, both of which are affected by fashion and the winds of change—though traditions of knowledge certainly exist in both.

Blake, in his notebooks, says, "Everything which is in harmony with me I call In harmony—But there may be things which are Not in harmony with Me & yet are in a More perfect Harmony."[4] This should narrow the writer's vision further, and Blake's proposition strikes across the honesty of a writer's intent as a qualitative measure. The proposition also implies that a reader must be willing to admit limitations in perspective. A more perfect harmony exists. Fifth Avenue at Christmas rush is exhilarating, but any city offers specific geophysical reference, especially when, as in New York, you enter ethnic or parochial, block-by-block neighborhoods.

I'll narrow this by being personal. In 1978, after living in a series of cities and rural areas in the East and Midwest of the United States and Canada, my family and I moved to North Dakota, my native state. We settled in the southwestern corner, three hundred miles from where I was born and lived until I was eight and then returned for a year of high school. But I had the feeling of returning home. And here might be the place to put to rest the sentimental supposition that you can't go home again. You may not be able to return to an earlier time but anybody can go back home, where "in folds of familiarity the land tighten[s] around," as Updike has put it in a semi-Oedipal conclusion to one of his short stories.[5] Where, after all, does one take one's rest, no matter how far one might travel from it, in every respect, except at home? Home is the center of rest, the wellspring of consciousness, the setting where our minds first open to light.

The definition of home or homeplace, and the implications of the locale we call home, is the matter I'm after. Is that home a haven? Is it a miniature heaven, a *picture* of heaven? Or is it hell?

The weight of my decision to move to North Dakota—it settled as a weight over my body—was not pleasant the first year. The weight was intellectual and emotional, centered on a concern for my family. Could they, would they, settle here? The possibility of their discontent was at times hellish. The geographical state we were living in wasn't quite the state I had once written about, which set off internal dislocations. What was I doing here, besides trying to reconcile a dozen discrepancies? As I searched for the cause of the weight, or my mistake, I came to several conclusions, and I'll use a few to define my subject from the inside—that itch along an arm under the armor.

I should say, first, that in an entirely other realm, the physical and psychic, I experienced a sense of healing integration I hadn't felt before, full blown and profound. The source of the weight started coming clear: it registered a commitment. I believe I'm a servant to my family, but I serve in another sense, too, and a servant's first allegiance is to his master. I don't serve myself or the academy per se, though I do teach, nor the place or populace of North Dakota. I serve God, through the person of Jesus as portrayed in the Bible. That should send a legion scurrying off in alarm or setting this aside in embarrassment—perhaps with the wish that I were a plain old regionalist and not a religionist, or whatever term you wish, and that suggests discrimination beneath the fear that leads to the categorizing reflex.

My spouse and I wanted to raise our children in the nurture and admonition Scripture encourages, in the country. We felt we were following the line of the covenant that began with Abraham and was reemphasized by the apostles (Acts 2:39)—that the promise of grace extended to us and to our children. That promise surpassed mere generational lines, which may be the reason I was uneasy about settling near my birthplace or the Red River valley where my great-grandparents homesteaded. The terms of the promise in the original pact aren't nullified or purified by the passage of time. If anybody wonders whether I believe those terms, or believe them to be true, the next question is, Do you believe Scripture, in its many ramifications? And I would have to say, yes, as far as I understand it, I do.

If I say from personal conviction and not in opposition to a doctrine or hermeneutic or philosopher's premise that nothing supernatural exists in the cosmos, I'm acknowledging that I've felt internal stirrings that suggest otherwise. That is, by speaking out of my conviction, without referring to any other teaching, I'm saying I carry inner information I wish to refute. That was my outlook for a decade as a writer. I worked to discredit in every way I could that internal evidence. My route was to accurately portray reality, I believed, which to me was unvarnished truth, no B.S. added, and over that route contravening evidence arrived. I can trace its path in Psalm 19 and the first chapter of the epistle to the Romans. In my ambition to refute that evidence, yet remain steadfast to my convictions and the characters in my fiction (for whom I'm also a servant), I see how my work began to build a case for the opposite side—affirming an overseeing autonomy, if not an affirmation of life itself.

If anybody thinks I've been deluded—an understandable response; I've held it—I feel I've been denied my search for the truth in the varieties of experience my work has brought about. We don't ask every existentialist if he or she has thought through every phase of belief to its outermost reaches, as Camus bravely did, and then near his end consulted with a pastor. It's obvious that many claim the right to a version of Camus's experience, and even if they undergo a certain amount of mental deliberation, and naturally angst, there's nothing original in their trek. That is why the verve and excitement of discovery is evaporating from American fiction.

The text that's the source of the Western tradition, the Bible, is frowned on if not scorned by many, so young writers have no fire to fight through, as Joyce and Camus and Colette and Tolstoy had to do. I know scholars who wouldn't think of criticizing *Ulysses* (either text) if they hadn't read it, but will gladly go at the Bible, unable to explain the difference between Ephesians and Ezekiel.

To suspect I've been deluded not only disallows the originality of the path that brought me here, but also ignores the tone and import of my early work—through *Beyond the Bedroom Wall*—when I seem, to my sense of it, to protest too much. This is a fine line that perhaps only I can detect, sensing it from the inside, and I should say that unless a standard exists against which beliefs can be measured, then every belief is equally valid (the common present-day belief) and modern currencies of belief may be based on mere social consensus or day-to-day trends, as they often are.

In the first sentence of *The Closing of the American Mind*, Allan Bloom states, "There is one thing a professor can be absolutely certain of: almost every student entering the university believes, or says he believes, that truth is relative."[6] Albert Einstein said, "The theory of relativity refers to physics, not morals."

Several matters intervened to suggest North Dakota as the place to head for. External confirmations occurred that can be seen as the concatenations of circumstance or working of Providence, however you wish, and I need to mention only two, and not in detail, to illustrate how we were urged in the direction we took. My wife and I spent several weeks traveling the West and Southwest, looking for a place to settle, and when we returned to Chicago, where we were living then, I asked her where she had most fully sensed the West, or the fresh air of a new place, and she said, "western North Dakota."

That was exactly what I felt, so her response was a surprise.

A denomination we decided to join had one church, we learned, in North Dakota. With a compass I drew a radius of forty miles, using the church as pivot point, and we found a farm within that circle. It was the sort of place we had looked for, in different regions of the country, for seven years, and it was in western North Dakota. I'm the fifth generation of my family to live in the state, my children the sixth, a minor feat—the state not a hundred years old when we moved. My great-grandparents settled in what was then Dakota Territory. We were far from there and my birthplace, as I've mentioned, and the farm was not handed down by the family, as often happens, through generations.

A larger promise was at work.

Those with roots in an immigrant background—a truism for many Americans—are prone to draw parallels with the Jews in their desert wanderings from Egypt, or to see the crossing of the ocean as their exodus. This is a temptation it's best to resist, since the Israelites were singled out to be freed from slavery—a picture of freedom from the death-dealing bondage of sin. Their exodus was brought to fruition for anybody who becomes a member of the household of God, grafted onto the root of Jesse into the original Israel. This can occur regardless of our nationality or race or gender or status or physical placement on this planet.

The Israelites claimed they were strangers and pilgrims on the earth, searching for a place of rest. About Abraham, the one in whose hands the promises of the covenant were placed, the epistle to the Hebrews says "he was looking forward to the city that has foundations, whose designer and builder is God" (11:10). That city sits on the cornerstone of the Word. "For here"—here on earth, the epistle says in its last chapter—"we have no lasting city, but we seek the city that is to come" (13:14). This is the heavenly Jerusalem and shouldn't dislocate us from our homework on earth. It's the life here we're responsible for, in its minutest detail. We should expect to give an account, according to a teaching of Jesus, for *every idle word* that comes out of our mouths. That's a weighty responsibility for a writer.

The responsibility began to increase in weight with our move to North Dakota. It's true that a prophet, and perhaps even a writer, is held in a certain amount of regard, except in his home state. No better temporal judges exist than family or friends who have known one from birth. With our move I now had neighbors, true critics, and was less able to fictionally fudge any sentence that appeared in my head or on a page. Many of my words, I felt, had indeed been idle, an acknowledgment that shifted me toward further accuracy. The commitment to a Lord and a church and a community might have carried me to this consciousness eventually, but the process was speeded up by the move. I started all over on a long novel half done, *Born Brothers.*

I say "might have carried me to this consciousness" because it is Scripture, as applied by the Spirit, that continues to refine for me the direction and meaning of home. A year before the move, I became (so I felt at the time), a believer; I began to read Scripture with the regularity I believed a believer should, and tended to believe it. In that sense, the Word *is* home.

If this seems formulaic or simplistic, so, too, does environmentalism at times to me, and I'm an environmentalist. If it seems like a sermon, at least it's not in a work of fiction, as excoriations of Christianity are, and the point is that standards and ethics, when open to hunches or common sense or reason, grow shaky as they move from our culture's home base. Western civilization took its shape from Scripture. With that gradient beneath my words, I don't have to set up a pulpit in a novel. My work has become more open ended, to the consternation of those who want explanations step by step, rather than accurate details, and it extends in freedom from a center of rest.

Graham Greene has written in his *Collected Essays* that "with the death of Henry James the religious sense was lost to the English novel, and with the religious sense went the sense of the importance of the human act."[7] Then this:

> The novelist, perhaps unconsciously aware of his predicament, took refuge in the subjective novel. . . . The visible world for him ceased to exist as completely as the spiritual. Mrs. Dalloway walking down Regent Street was aware of the glitter of shop-windows, the smooth passage of cars, the conversation of shoppers, but it was only a Regent Street seen by Mrs. Dalloway that was conveyed to the reader: a charming whimsical rather sentimental prose poem was what Regent Street had become; a current of air, a touch of scent, a sparkle of glass. But, we protest, Regent Street too has a right to exist; it is more real than Mrs. Dalloway.[8]

This subjective mode that readers discover in many modern novels limits the world to the filtering consciousness of one person rather than a first or limited third person, and imprisons the natural world and its people. The viewpoint never explores manifestations of reality that can take language deeper than before. The earth groans for redemption, as we do, while it promises an eternal renewal we share, at least suggestively, in nature's cycles—spring springing green again. The caliber of an open consciousness can take in a strawberry and its complexity of texture, not to say the act of eating its humped and seedy yet vermillion-sweet spillage of—I fumble for words.

Rapture is the primary matter I hope to fumble over. It's my responsibility to elevate consciousness by rendering the interlocking nature of the "things of this world," as Richard Wilbur puts it, including our lives within it, good or bad, in their manifold specifics—by reconstructing, through language, a niche of existence a reader can rest in. If I can't lead a young person through the minefield of the world, I'm blindly leading the blind. And if I take a leap of faith into a nameless dark, it's to discern light's source, a matter of good news, as long as I can reconcile the metaphor of language with the changing yet essentially unchangeable, actual, fallen world.

As an analogue to my odyssey of reconciliation, I offer a commentary by Wendell Berry on the original *Odyssey*. In his fiction and nonfiction, Berry is the wisest and most articulate American writer about "place" and the meaning of home, and he says of Odysseus in "The Body and the Earth," from *Recollected Essays*, that his "far-wandering through the wilderness of the sea is not merely the return of a husband; it is a journey home."[9]

> By the end of Book XXIII, it is clear that the action of the narrative, Odysseus' journey from the cave of Kalypso to the bed of Penelope, has revealed a structure that is at once geographical and moral. This structure may be graphed as a series of diminishing circles centered on one of the posts of the marriage bed. Odysseus makes his way from the periphery toward that center. . . . As he moves toward this center he moves also through a series of recognitions, tests of identity, and devotion. By these, his homecoming becomes at the same time a restoration of order.[10]

One way in which Odysseus restores order, grimly, is by slaughtering Penelope's suitors, and of this Berry says, "The suitors' sin is their utter contempt for the domestic order that the poem affirms."[11] The entire Trojan War began, indeed, when a guest took advantage of the hospitality required of a Greek host.

> For Odysseus, then, marriage was not merely a legal bond, nor even a sacred bond, between himself and Penelope. It was part of a complex practical circumstance involving, in addition to husband and wife, their family, both descendants and forebears, their household, their community, and the sources of all these lives in memory and tradition, in the countryside, and in the earth.[12]

My return to North Dakota sought a similar order. I was raised and catechized in the Catholic Church and knew its doctrines from childhood. A bombardment of unbelief in college dismantled my faith, because I had little to refer to other than the catechism and the traditions of the church. For some that community and communion might have been enough, and it might have been for me, too, at another time. But not then.

In times of crisis I prayed, no matter what I was pretending or saying or not saying about belief. I gave thanks for passages of prose beyond my capabilities, aware that they couldn't have arrived wholly from the often fractured state of my consciousness. When I was writing *Beyond the Bedroom Wall*, I began to read the Bible in order to understand the certainties previous generations had upheld, and most of the doctrines that had been catechized into me were confirmed.

A series of verses, especially in Ephesians—"even as he chose us in him before the foundation of the world, that we should be holy and blameless before him"—coalesced. A span broad as the cosmos seemed to overarch my life, now that that life had been acted upon and restored, forward to back. I understood the power of grace. Though I lived in unbelief, denied God and cursed him, he kept his side and called me back. I was, in the truest sense, home. And in my new geophysical state I could be more accurate, as I discovered in *Born Brothers*, about a place and a people I was in communion with.

If values evolve from traditions and common sense, then when values start clashing, we need a judge or referee, as we do when we turn to a dictionary to define words. Otherwise any individual value is as valid as another. Without an outside guide we're in Babel, where everybody is talking nonsense, because everybody is using words that have meaning only to themselves, and, as Einstein has pointed out, "It is easier to denature plutonium than to denature the basic evil nature of man."

The best source to teach us about this nature realistically, and why it exists as it does, is the Word. It's the fixed pivot on which this world revolves. If a person moves from that pivot or spirals away from it, as I have, "the heavens over your head shall be bronze, and the earth under you shall be iron," as in Deuteronomy 28:23.

A metallic, unfeeling universe with a lid over every avenue upward is not an enviable existence. It can sober a writer about the necessity of one-mindedness in the search for reconciliation, as with Esau, who "found no chance to repent, though he sought it with tears." It conveys a sense of the separation I underwent, and I now know that every person on earth is spared the entirety of that separation, though some will be left, eventually, by the wayside. I, with my contrary nature, need to be reminded of that to avoid the rebellion of separation for separation's sake—freedom, as I once called it. For those whose heaven is brass and the earth iron, any home here is hell.

Writers who seek direction are admonished by the eighth verse in the last chapter of the epistle to the Philippians, which is a list. Lists in Scripture often run in descending order of importance (though not always), and here it says, "Whatever is *true*"—an admonition to not remake matters in order to pretty them up—"whatever is honorable, whatever is *just*"—justice, especially of a spiritual sort, isn't easy to accept with an honorable spirit—"whatever is *pure*, whatever is *lovely*, whatever is commendable"—whatever is excellent or praiseworthy in these, we're to think of that. Yes, I affirm, but we need to keep it all in proper balance, and the place to begin is with truth.

The realism of the world the Word reveals is not a goody-two-shoes kind. We read about incest, prostitution, giving up a daughter as a living sacrifice due to a vain vow, adultery, hate, murder, as in driving a tent stake through a warrior's head after lying to him. So we don't need to pretend that some soulful form of sanitized Victorianism was the state of mind of the authors or Author of such passages. If the realism of the Word exposes realities sometimes shocking or emotionally loaded, seeming a bitter pill to swallow, we should expect similarities in our everyday existence, as it was with Jesus. We may search for the invisible in faith, forever propelled forward, but also have the business of the world to be about, the bare brute reality of it.

I should be able to describe a patch of ground so faithfully that you would know it if you came upon it (imaginative fantasies of moonscapes won't do), and could traverse it if you had to, with no hazard to your life. To do less for the interior landscape of a woman or man or child, or the pitfalls the world presents to them, is irresponsible. If my prose sets before you a naked person, as church painters do, in a representation of his or her beauty, or to remind you of its pitfalls, and I've done all I can to keep the image from being a temptation, I'm able to say I've presented something pure and beautiful, so why do your thoughts run in another direction?

Writers may be reformers after they reform themselves and their outlook, but they aren't *re*formers if they aren't shaping contemporary experience and phenomena into forms that illustrate a dependence on, and captivity to, ultimate form. Chaos can't be illustrated without order to depart from, and it's up to writers, as it's been for centuries, to help us find our way around this home on earth, whatever our place on it.

Christian writers, especially, should be suggesting directions for our culture, as they have since Shakespeare, rather than scrambling backward to find favor with whatever "readership." If I merely sit in a pew once a week, content to rest in the patriarchal embrace of previous believers or, worse, if I'm self-satisfied and smug, my faith and works are dying on the vine, if not long-past dead. I've placed a burden on the backs of my children that won't be easy or light, and left work undone for them to undertake. So if I shy from describing the worst winter landscape or a person as that person epitomizes the truth, that is, if I retreat into the arena of false prudery or the social consensus of what some might term *taste*, which is not in the list above and is as changeable as clothes, then somebody may never be able to make their way through that inscape, and I've lied to you and my children—the little ones I'm not to offend. This is the literal hell of any writer.

Children are called out, too, to lead lives in a world that it is my duty to portray with accuracy and passion—this planet, this earth, this precious place spinning through its fixed purposes each hour. I reach from my armor to that generation, as I reach to you, reader, to say we are sanctified by Truth. That Truth is accessible to all and exists forever as our enfolding home.

3

VIEWS OF WENDELL BERRY

On Life against Agribusiness

One of the rewards of being a fairly faithful reader arrives when you open a book and realize it's the one you've been reading toward for years. This was my experience with the work of Wendell Berry, when I encountered *The Gift of Good Land* and *Recollected Essays* in the early eighties. Berry's name was familiar to me, from his poetry and a brief piece or two in *The Whole Earth Catalogue*, I assume, since I missed all five of the collections gathered in *Recollected Essays*.[1] As a reader, one wonders about the vagaries of self and circumstance that cause such an oversight, but on this occasion, now that the reading has led me to Berry's work, the proper response is gratitude.

His essays are the sort to spend weeks with and return to often. There is that much pleasure in them, both in the surety of the prose and the breadth and depth of content. They are true reference works and books of practical help for anybody who cares about the earth and the quality of life on it. That should include us all, and especially those who live in the landlocked stretches of inland America.

Berry doesn't practice the worshipful environmentalism that is the religion of many Americans who never contend with nature. He has lived on and worked the land; he knows the cost. Some of his best essays date from the sixties (and a few bear the imprint of that time) but more recent exquisite collections, *Standing by Words* and *What Are People For?* were written over the Reagan years, and *Sex, Economy, Freedom & Community* appeared in 1993. The new books represent the essential ideas of the early essays with a newly thought-through clarity of integration. Certain passages and paragraphs have the power to lift you into stretches of contemplation and personal reassessment—those periods when you seem to be staring out a window but are really assessing the realignment your consciousness is taking on. Berry's books are that well built and keep revealing new dimensions.

His central focus is the land, or *agriculture*, with equal emphasis on both halves of that word, because he writes not only of land and animal husbandry, but of industrialization and "agribusiness," the youth movement of the sixties, the family, the Reagan years, contemporary education and the lack of it, politics and government, his refusal to use a computer, the search for a suitable pastor to serve a rural Kentucky congregation, and on into ever-widening realms, which is as it should be. All of this is the culture that *agri* supports. Without the land, not one cultural endeavor could exist, as Berry understands.

Nobody would. This is an unalterable truth that seems to have evaporated from every urban area, meaning most of America, in our time. Berry asks us to consider how we imagine we eat, for example, when the consciousness of dependence on farmers has been wiped from our minds. I once asked a group of undergraduates from the East where their food came from, and they said, with unblinking authority, the deli. Come on, I said. "OK, stores." The farthest their imagination could reach was "warehouses." This lack of education is another of Berry's concerns.

His approach is the opposite of shrill and slapdash, as anyone who enters the prose of *Recollected Essays* or *Sex, Economy, Freedom & Community* or *What Are People For?* will discover. It is prose that moves at the pace of the natural world and slows us so we're able to study that world in the detail it deserves. Berry began with himself. Forty years ago, after spending a decade as a poet-traveler and professor, he moved with his wife and two children to a small acreage in upper Kentucky, near Port Royal, which had been in his family for generations; it was in Port Royal that Berry was born and grew up. He returned and grew back into the area, or as much as that is possible for a twentieth-century person to do, and a discerning, literary one at that, with the distancing medium of language always an aggravation. His act of return should put to rest for good the absurd supposition that you can't go home again.

In "The Long-Legged House," one of the first of the recollected or rethought-through essays, and the following "A Native Hill," he examines the reasons for his move. A quiet purl of self-evaluation and steady daily work extends from here and concludes in "The Making of a Marginal Farm," a modern success story of the most humble and revolutionary sort. On a sloping riverside farm of seventy acres, Berry has begun to show a profit.

In "Damage" and "Healing" from the later *What Are People For?*, he confesses the mistake he made in dredging out a portion of a hillside to create a pond for watering livestock, and the ways in which the land (and Berry, the damager) have since been healed. A single paragraph from "Healing" should be on every writer's wall: "A creature is not a creator, and cannot be. There is only one Creation, and we are its members."[2] Most contemporary writers have foregone this creature-Creator distinction for the neo-Romantic fantasy of being creator gods.

Only what lies before Berry, or affects his life, is spoken of in his low-key, reasoning tone. He is not a speculative seer or a specialist. He has been called a prophet of our times and "prophetic" by reviewers, but would probably demur to the biblical definition of that word, or say, simply, "I'm not." He's seen by some who are confined to cities as a person who has "gone back to the land," and referred to by others (with that slur of condescension) as a regionalist. Although he writes about a specific region, he is no more a regionalist than Aesop; he's a poet.

He makes no special claims for himself and any limits imposed on him could well reflect the reader's flawed tendency toward pigeonholing—that characteristic that computers (Berry hates them) epitomize. If he can be seen as a prophet it would be in a broader sense; he is pleading from his home territory for a change in people in general. His power lies in his refusal to reach beyond what he knows. But his flair for knowing what he knows in all its earthly interconnections will affect you as though you are being seen into.

By not only remaining still but retreating, even, into the lives of his ancestors, Berry has entered that curious process of growing away from expected intellectual formulations and classifications— those contemporary attitudes that strike us as familiar but are merely modish. The precision of his thought suggests an integrated whole, as here: "Respect, I think, always implies imagination—the ability to see one another, across our inevitable differences, as living souls."[3] He speaks with immediacy but as if out of the ages, and as a man of wisdom and acumen, and as a writer, he stands alone.

He has been compared to Thoreau, but Berry has a commitment to community uncongenial to Thoreau. The idealistic gaze (or glaze) of Transcendentalism has been transformed in Berry into the vision of a concerned parent searching for the relevant applications for a child who will soon be facing the same world—the sort of person who has the practical sense to shade his eyes by wearing a cap.

Besides pages of specific notes, I've come from the essays with a memory of passages that contain some of the most tender and unselfish, and unembarrassed, expressions I've read of a husband's love for his wife; a feeling of having had captured, with the rhythms and clarity of unaffected language, the fall of a wild stream or a leisurely walk in the morning through familiar woods; the pleasure of encountering one of the most sound and searching analyses of the hippie generation of the sixties, bracketed by the wonderful title that itself suggests a solution to the antipathies of that time, "Discipline and Hope."[4] And I have a clearer perspective on the folly of farmers in their attempts to impose their conception of order on the land before they've bothered to examine the order inherent in it, being what it is, a creation separate from them—that hubristic attitude in which we see nature as an extension of ourselves, or worse, a passive goddess or Mother-Nature-Gaia to be slapped into shape to serve our ends or mounted with whirligigs of wind power, as if our additions will appreciably lessen her immense natural modulations in climate and temperature—and by this I don't mean I'm a troglodyte; I have both wind and solar power and a wood-burning furnace on an organic farm.

Even when Berry writes about industry and the depredations of a government that creates "leisure-areas" by dismantling or burying under water great tracts of wilderness while displacing hundreds and thousands of people who will need more leisure-areas, he somehow manages not to spill into mere anger or the spittle-charged polemics of the religion of contemporary politics—especially after the latest presidential election. The heat of indignation rises through his prose, but finally the prose is able to remain irenic.

If I had to distill the import of his thought, I might put it like this: all land is a gift, and all of it is good, if we only had the sensibility to see that. Again making no claims for himself, Berry functions not only as our eyes but also as an entire body and intelligence responding to the land, and it's a response few will return from unmoved. He refers to Sir Albert Howard's premise that in order for man to understand the farm, and the other cleared spaces he's created, he must return to the woods, and writes: "His life will grow out of the ground like the other lives of the place, and take its place among them. He will be with them—neither ignorant of them, nor indifferent to them, nor against them—and so at last he will grow to be native-born. That is, he must reenter the silence and the darkness, and be born again."[5]

This is from an essay first published in 1969, before Jimmy

Carter and Charles Colson (and after them, media evangelists) helped popularize that phrase into the kicking dog it's become. Berry is asking for the same sort of total transformation, or change of heart, as when, near the conclusion of the same essay, he says, "It is not from ourselves that we will learn to be better than we are."[6]

He suggests that the only true education we may ever receive is from the natural world (or "the creation," as he calls it in the earlier essays, and which in the later ones evolves to "Creation") in all of its unclassifiable mystery, and that we won't begin to understand it until we admit that in its totality it is, indeed, incomprehensible. In the later "Christianity and the Survival of Creation," a sort of sermon given at a Southern Baptist seminary, Berry seems to merge immanence—the Creator everywhere present in creation, with pantheism—the Creator inherently *in* creation's every element.[7] But this is a rather technical theological fine point, and it is better to err this way, to my mind, in the direction of reverence, than toward deism—the Creator absent, absconded, after having set the intricate mechanism (*organic*, of course) in place, and wound its mainspring tight.

A glimpse of Berry's view of the mystery of creation is apparent in "Woods," one of the poems from *A Part*, his fifteenth book of poetry:

> I part the out thrusting branches
> and come in beneath
> the blessed and blessing trees.
> Though I am silent
> there is singing around me.
> Though I am dark
> there is vision around me.
> Though I am heavy
> there is flight around me.[8]

Poetry's province is to express with concision the spirit, whether it's the spirit of the poet fashioning it, or the animating spirit that a particular poet discerns in life, and in this instance I don't sense a case being made for primitivism. Of Berry's books of poetry, *A Part*, along with *Sabbaths*, helps supply the governance of his perspective. And for those who say that they have trouble understanding modern poetry, I offer, along with the above, the following complete poem:

> Instead of reading Chairman Mao
> I think I'll go and milk my cow.[9]

Though not to imply that the matter Berry covers in his poetry is simple or, worse, simplistic—on the contrary, considering the implications of both of the above. Rather, Berry has been brought to an understanding of his place in nature and has achieved a rapprochement with it that hasn't been seen in American poetry or expressed with such directness, perhaps, since Robert Frost.

Of the books of essays, *Recollected Essays* unfolds for me with the most poetic density, as is natural, since it formulates the pith of Berry's convictions; and a person of his sort can make the commitment and move he has made only once. The prose falls in clear and full thoughts: "A political speech made on television has to be first and last a show, simply because it has no chance to be anything else. The great sin of the medium is not that it presents fiction as truth, as undoubtedly it sometimes does, but that it cannot help presenting the truth as fiction."[10] Or, "Freedom is a personal matter; though we may be enslaved as a group, we can be free only as persons."[11] And "The most destructive of ideas is that extraordinary times justify extraordinary measures. This is the ultimate relativism. . . . Thus the violent have always rationalized their violence."[12] Finally, "Ways of life change only in living. To live by expert advice is to abandon one's life."[13]

The pieces collected in *The Gift of Good Land*, most of which were written for magazine publication, are slightly thinner but are in the best practical sense (that of relating to affairs of community and state) more useful. This is also true of the essays in *Home Economics* and *What Are People For?*—a title that echoes, consciously or not, Francis Schaeffer's *Whatever Happened to the Human Race?* The essays in these books are accounts of the actual working out of Berry's ideas in application to his life on the land and life in general. And in *What Are People For?* and *Sex, Economy, Freedom & Community* his applications achieve the integrated finality I've mentioned.

If someone is looking for immediate answers to questions about actual life on the land, rather than theories about it, the four books above are the ones to look into. It's a way of life that works wondrously well, one learns, in pockets of this country—for the Amish, for instance, who buy up eighty acres of burnt-out soil and soon have it supporting an entire family—or on the ashy soil of portions of Central America, as it has for centuries.

It is life as life was meant to be lived, and was and is lived, still, in spite of experts who say it won't work and are ready with ag-school theories. Berry sets out in detail, especially in *The Gift of Good Land* and *What Are People For?*, the different kinds of death and destruction that ag-school and government and "professional" advice have caused across America, and will continue to cause on its own momentum. But the reader comes away from his books with hope, as a result of his stand, and as a result of an acquaintance, through Berry, with others taking a similar stand. And hope, too, in a larger sense, for this stripped and damned and befouled planet that in spite of our insults continues to sustain its balance of life among the galaxies stretching off from it in their different degrees of burning or frigid infecundity. Our hope is here on earth. And here is a human being speaking with calm and sanity out of its cultivated hills into the technological wilderness closing in on all sides. We would do well to hear him.

*   *   *

I want to add some comments on Berry's publisher, first known as North Point Press, then Counterpoint, and then (revealing the man behind this procession) Shoemaker-Hoard, and now yet again Counterpoint. From its beginnings, this publisher has echoed

Berry's concerns—a happy circumstance for a writer. North Point entered publishing as an independent (not controlled by a conglomerate, or owned by a television network or oil company or German corporation, as all New York houses now are) with a mailing address in Berkeley, California. Its offices were in a near suburb, largely run by one person, Jack Shoemaker. It was one of the first houses to settle in California, and perhaps sparked a migration, as houses such as Harcourt, Brace, Berry's former publisher, moved from New York to escape the can of worms metaphor coined by Hemingway that has plagued the industry. And so a division of Harper & Row (now HarperCollins) has settled in San Francisco Bay as HarperSanFrancisco.

North Point began by reissuing out-of-print books of merit by writers such as Berry, Guy Davenport, and Evan Connell, and also instituting its own list of fiction; its own list of poetry, essays, and translations by these and other writers—novels from Gilbert Sorrentino and Ross Feld, for example. All North Point books had Smythe-sewn bindings, as was true of nearly all hardbacks until thirty years ago, before the advent of perfect, or glued, bindings (previously used only on paperbacks)—perfection that has a tendency to explode with a crack down its center when you open one wide. So went my *Humboldt's Gift* in the year Bellow won the Nobel. North Point issued their books simultaneously in both hardback and paper.

These were trade paperbacks, the type and page size the same as the hardbacks, and were also Smythe sewn and had elegant dust jackets. This is the only way that most books in France and Sweden and other European countries are produced and issued. They have a smart, durable feel—a design that American publishers might eventually have to turn to (no more hardbacks at all, except perhaps for reference) if they plan to keep book prices within reach of the average reader. All of North Point's Berry books were exemplars of the fading art of craftsmanlike book construction and so are actual artifacts, as I suspect most books will soon be, considering the

Kindle, the iPad, and a variety of electronic readers which, however, deliver only an *image* of print.

There was obviously a far-sighted plan to issue Berry's work in a uniform edition, with contrasting cloth on each spine harmonizing with the cover color, the books of a small portable size the late Edmund Wilson used to favor. American publishing in general lacks this organized and sympathetic overview, which in the past was a publisher's way of indicating confidence in a writer's future. Berry's books were tastefully designed, the perfect shape to hold and handle. They would lie open on their backs for easy reference, without that disrupting eruption down the center that means your twenty-five- or thirty-dollar book is ruined and will soon start shedding pages from both sides of the fracture. North Point books were printed with brown-tinted ink on off-white, acid-free paper, which doesn't reflect light into the back of your head, even under strong illumination. A few of the books of poetry are gems, about the width of a hand, or the overall size of a European wallet, with a woodcut on their red-brown dust jackets, and, in the paperback versions, a pristine white jacket (conforming to the design of the other Berry paperbacks) with title and author in silver print.

The acid-free paper ensures relative permanence. Since the mid-1800s, when acid-deteriorated pulp was substituted for cloth content in book paper, books have had self-destruction built into them. The acid content causes a brittle decomposition, hastened by exposure to the air (and especially to polluted air), that at first begins to darken the edges of a book's pages. I see this happening to older books on my shelves. The paper is literally eating itself up. The process in its onset becomes visible when you let a newspaper lie in the open for a few days—the cheaper the paper, the quicker it darkens. This has created a problem that libraries and archivists are trying to keep up with by controlled environments and microfiche and computer storage. Collectors would do well to look for Smythe-sewn bindings and acid-free paper in books they buy for investments, and consider themselves fortunate if they find both together in one contemporary book out of a thousand.

For my demurrers, there were times during my readings of Berry when it seemed he would have been better served, considering the quality of his prose and its concerns, by a typeface with not quite such a formal and modern, mechanical feel as the Mergenthaler Sabon all his North Point books were set in—employing some form of the CPR or photosetting process. The exact regularity after some six-hundred pages of essayist's prose, no matter how admirable that essayist, tends to be lulling, without the exciting, graphic, *made* texture, indicating the presence of a human hand, that's visible in the linotype process, even when photo-reproduced. On the other hand, Mergenthaler Sabon's crispness is apt and tends to fade under the substance of Berry's thought in a way that a more showy or ornate type wouldn't.

The Gift of Good Land, the second volume of essays, has a glue-impregnated feel to its cloth, as if North Point had already begun to cut back. And this and *Recollected Essays*, issued the same year, arrived with excess glue squeezed from the tops of their spines, so the edges of outer pages adhered to the droplets, which I had to pick off to prevent the stuck-together pages from tearing—as if the bindery has to learn (or relearn) that sewn signatures need only enough glue to hold the endpapers in place, not the entire spine, as in perfect binding. In some of North Point's later volumes, this flaw seems to have been corrected.

These are anyway petty quibbles in the face of overall excellence, and it was heartening to see a publisher take the care North Point did for its writers and its product. Whether North Point would ever ascend to the heavens of the independents such as Covici-Friede, the former Alfred A. Knopf (before it was merged with Random House-Pantheon-Vintage, etc., themselves under a larger conglomerate), or the present Farrar, Straus and Giroux is a question that will never be resolved (and Farrar, Straus is now no longer independent) because North Point went belly up and was bought out by Farrar, Straus. Some of North Point's backlist moved to Pantheon, a division of Random House, within *its* conglomerate, and Berry moved to Pantheon at that time.

Jack Shoemaker started Counterpoint Press, which published more Berry books, and then Counterpoint apparently went belly up and was bought out by the Perseus Group, one of the few semi-independent publishers remaining. Shoemaker then started Shoemaker-Hoard, and recently bought Counterpoint back from Perseus.

All of this should remind us, as Berry reminds us, to think small, not big. And to perhaps hold foremost the truth that we're all at the mercy of time, that eventual sifter of the elements of every history, whether written large or small across the decomposing substance of the present.

4

Am Lit

On a Writer's Incorrect Views

John Gardner's posthumous collection of nonfiction, *On Writers and Writing*, has been reissued in trade paperback by Addison-Wesley, who earlier brought out the hardback.[1] In his introduction to the collection, the NBA-winning novelist and MacArthur Fellow, Charles Johnson, begins with this sentence:

> On the day of his fatal motorcycle accident on September 14, 1982, on a lonely though not particularly dangerous curving stretch of road in Susquehanna County, Pennsylvania, John Gardner, the embattled advocate for higher artistic and moral standards in our fiction, was snatched at age forty-nine from the stage of contemporary American literature before we could properly measure either his contribution to literary culture or the man himself.[2]

Johnson was a student and friend, indebted to Gardner as a Zen adept is to a master, and thus his tone. But the curve of his sentence suggests the direction that future writing about Gardner will take: an embattled and romantic literary figure of Byronic dimensions, one with standards, has been snatched away at the height of his powers, before proper assessment has been made of "either his contribution to literary culture or the man himself."

True assessment, of course, centers on a writer's work. Time is never kind to "the man himself," as Johnson knows, and the more facts that exist about a writer, the more those facts are assembled, it seems, to suit an assessor's ends. Better that nobody knows you, or that intimates are absent when the assessment begins, as with Will-from-on-Avon. Besides, in our age of information overload, when facts seem to breed further facts and every person is a creative biographer, à la the new historicism or, worse, the Internet, or, worst of all, a blog, it's unsettling to view the assessments the meanest daily manufacture.

But Johnson has mentioned literary culture and "the man himself" for a reason. The shock waves caused by Gardner's death were due to the gravity of his personality and the mystery of the accident that took his life. Those affected by Gardner are never neutral about him; it's either love or hate. Or, if not exactly hate, disdain for him as a self-anointed meddler in literary currents of correctness in the manner of an Old Testament prophet. This view of him gained ascendency when *On Moral Fiction* appeared in 1976, with a large percentage of "literary culture" howling in outrage, "*Who does this guy think he is?* He's so outré he says fiction has a moral basis—his excuse for letting fly at postmodernists!"

Gardner fashioned the persona of a durable if not cultic figure who, for over a decade, seemed omnipresent. It's no surprise that biographies of him are out and that he's been incorporated in memoirs, but I believe his own ideas, as expressed in these essays, are a better way of getting at the person he was. Here in his words are the actual statements, incisive and measured and sometimes outrageous, that registered his presence. Many of those who continue to love him, with a passion and staying power few writers seem able to inspire, are former students, but by no means all; others "discovered" Gardner, as they reckon it, in one or another of his novels.

Gardner was one of the early creative writing gurus, and, as a teacher of writing, can hardly be bettered. His *Art of Fiction* and

On Becoming a Novelist are still the most helpful books available to aspiring writers, and those who heard Gardner speak these words in workshops tend, as I've suggested, to revere him. As editor of *MSS* and an obliging correspondent whose letters sometimes ran longer than a submitted story, and as a mentor, he jogged along so many writers the numbers probably run into the thousands. One of prominence is Raymond Carver, and there was never a time in Carver's life when he didn't acknowledge with gratitude Gardner's encouragement and direction. Another is Charles Johnson.

As a critic, Gardner kept his square, strong farmer's hand firmly on the pulse of American fiction, and you either waited for or feared his reviews and assessments of writers and writing—his manifestos, as they were seen by some, diatribes and hallucinations by others. Here I should mention that I write not only as an observer of Gardner and one reviewed by him, but as one of those, along with Galway Kinnell and others, invited to help fill the vacuum at Binghamton after Gardner's death. I have observed the lonely stretch of curving road in Susquehanna County Johnson describes. I've spent time with both of Gardner's widows (he was married twice) and with the young graduate student he intended to marry the week of his accident. I eventually taught the graduate students from different corners of the country who had come to Binghamton to write a novel under Gardner's direction.

His life indeed contained romantic elements, hints of which Johnson conveys in his introduction. Gardner was a farm boy, unabashedly so, and usually lived in a rural setting with his family and a menagerie of animals. Before he began to favor denim work shirts, he wore a medieval leather jerkin or a black leather motorcycle jacket. Some adherents and students and fans (yes, he had fans) tried to imitate his lifestyle or manner of dress, but none could manage his actual presence, with white-blond hair to his shoulders and the disarming aura of a shining angel. He could be so unassuming and stolid you wondered where the words for "An Invective Against Mere Fiction"—one of the essays collected here—originated.

Yet others viewed him as the bad boy of literature. He was called this (and less flattering names) by those who didn't take to him or saw him as a self-aggrandizing interloper. He drank too much and didn't hang out with the right crowd, meaning those in New York; he tended to admire writers whose names you might have to have repeated; he was unsparing about overrated popular writers (he usually called them "fashionable," with a sneer you could detect); he drove a Harley hog or a Mercedes or a VW, and was not always modest. He spoke unabashedly about himself and his work. He was as well read as any writer alive at the time, a polymath who could talk knowledgeably not only about fiction, past or foreign or contemporary, but music, theology, philosophy, history, physics—most any topic that came up.

He didn't merely hold forth, though he could do that; his talk was laced with references from books that even some of the experts in the fields hadn't read, and his ability to quote verbatim swatches from pages suggested a memory nearly photographic. At other times he was a musing or amused listener, moving his pipe around in his mouth as he sat back dreamily silent. The pipe was both a pleasure and a prop. He smoked most anything within reach but tended to return to the pipe. You can sense him sliding it over his teeth or puffing away at it and then biting down as he zeros in on the right word in the sentences of these essays.

He also wrote fiction, and two of his novels were bestsellers. Most of his fiction traveled traditional routes, but one boot of Gardner (Wellingtons, usually) was planted in postmodernism as surely as the other bore traces Of The Farm near Batavia, New York, where he grew up. His experimental range includes *Grendel*, *The Sunlight Dialogues*, *In the Suicide Mountains*, and *Freddy's Book*, and his more traditional novels (and to my taste better) are *Nickel Mountain*, *Mickelsson's Ghosts*, and the central narrative portions of *October Light*. He wrote a book-length poem, two short story collections, several children's books, and a biography of Chaucer—over twenty books in all before his motorcycle went out of control on that curve.

On that sunlit September afternoon, Gardner was on his way to Binghamton for yet another conference with a student, carrying manuscripts in his motorcycle carrier. Contrary to rumors, he had not been drinking heavily or otherwise acting suicidal, as those closest to him at that time report. He was working on a new novel, had recovered from the negative reviews of *Mickelsson's Ghosts*, had recently written a friend about a translation of *Gilgamesh* he was finishing with another friend— "Great pome!"—and was looking forward to getting married that weekend with his usual sunny disposition. The curve was elementary for a seasoned motorcyclist, and someone who lived in a farmhouse on a hill near the curve said she heard a noise and then saw a pickup speeding away, so perhaps Gardner was forced off the road by a local. Or he could have been daydreaming too deeply; his memorable definition of fiction was "the vivid and continuous dream."[3] When his motorcycle went down, the end of a handlebar ruptured his spleen. There wasn't a mark on his body. The pickup couldn't be traced. He remains as romantic and enigmatic in death as in life.

There has been no hurry, it seems, to assess Gardner's work, and perhaps *On Writers and Writing* is a place to begin. In "More Smog from the Dark Satanic Mills," Gardner laments the fashionable trash and imitation serious fiction that obscures first-rate writing, and suggests, in an amusing scenario, that perhaps editors don't really read the books they publish:

> They buy the novel from an agent who has never read it either, he just "represents" it, the way a number can represent two sick fish or two chickenhouses, and to get them to buy it the agent throws in some other novel, cheaper than it would have been otherwise,

by someone like John Hersey, who's safe. The editor gives the manuscript to a girl from Radcliffe, who fixes the spelling and changes the parts that aren't clear to her, and then somebody else who's read twenty-five pages writes the jacket blurb which vaguely alludes to "outrageous humor" or "delicate insight" and the "deeper symbolic intent."[4]

Gardner was not a humorless academic. Readers will find a release of pleasure in nearly every essay or review collected here, whether of Cheever or Lewis Carroll or John Steinbeck or Italo Calvino or John Fowles. When Gardner reviewed a particular writer, or addressed a topic as broad as "Contemporary American Fiction," as he does here, he came to his subject prepared, often with months of reading behind him, and with a larger context in which to assess the contemporary nature or not of the writers he was considering. A few references in the essays might seem slightly dated, but his insights are always arresting: "I happen to know that Joyce Carol Oates, the goriest writer in America, shuts her eyes during the bloody parts of Polanski's *Macbeth*."[5]
About Tolkien:

His edition of *Sir Gawain and the Green Knight* was a good, trustworthy edition, not brilliant—curiously weak when it comes to interpretation—and his modernizations of that poem and also of *Pearl* and *Sir Orfeo* were loaded with forced inversions, false rhymes and silly archaisms like "eke" and "ere." Tolkien's original story-poems, like "The Adventures of Tom Bombadil," were even worse, yet *The Lord of the Rings* looms already as one of the truly great works of the human spirit.[6]

I haven't mentioned Gardner's wide reading and study in medieval literature, or his book on Chaucer's poetics, the genesis of which he mentions here:

At the Iowa Writer's Workshop, where, like Flannery O'Connor and everybody else, I'd gone to study my trade, I'd arrived too late and so encountered not the great white company of earlier days but Freudian novelist Marguerite Young, sodbuster Robert

O'Bowen, and wooden allegorists like Calvin Kentfield, writers of the sort who, to set us yawning, divide their books about life in the Navy into sections entitled Earth, Air, Fire, and Water. . . . I quit the writer's workshop and went up the hill to take classes in Italian, Greek, and Latin, to John McGalliard's Old English Class, where people still cared about stories.[7]

If you pity the poor sodbuster or allegorist who got in Gardner's way, notice how fast they've faded: fashionable. Yet Gardner's statement above could be construed as misleading. He did become competent in several languages and eventually translated from more than one and, yes, was as well read in medieval literature as most scholars in the field and did write about Chaucer, but both his master's degree and his doctorate, as the records show, were in creative writing. Even his biography of Chaucer caused a critical flurry or furor when it appeared, with certain scholars claiming it contained unacknowledged borrowings, if not outright plagiarism.

But Gardner was most cogent on the contemporary scene. He notes of Barthelme (and in particular *Snow White*) that Barthelme's work

has nothing to do with black comedy—Beckett's *Happy Days*, for instance, which angrily laughs at brainless optimism. . . . Like Ralph Waldo Emerson ("I contradict myself?"), Barthelme's crazies systematically evade the issue, and they encourage the reader to evade it too, with neurotically healthy vigor. They work like the Christianity of those Updike adults who have shucked religion but carry on from childhood a security ultimately untouched by their knowledge that it's groundless.[8]

This is from his essay "Contemporary American Fiction," a brilliant cataract of twenty-five pages that includes most American writers of the era. Gardner states his premise early on: "Though most of the writers I plan to mention would dislike my calling them religious, American writers now at work fall into five main groups: (1) religious liberals and liberal agnostics (often indistinguishable); (2) orthodox or troubled-orthodox Christians; (3) Christians who have lost their faith and cannot stand it; (4) diabolists; (5) heretics."[9]

About the liberals, he says with insight:

> From Emerson to Saul Bellow the line runs straight. The Reform Jew is only barely a Jew, as the Transcendentalist is only barely a Christian. He believes in ethics and civilization, tradition and clear communication. When he writes he uses plot, character, and setting, and he's fairly true to all of them, to prove—in case anyone should doubt—that he's serious. He does not believe, if you press him, in art. He believes in using art to facilitate thought about important issues.[10]

Some of the writers other than Bellow that Gardner gathers under this rubric are Elkin, Mailer, and Malamud. Gardner notes that "Except for Walt Whitman, the liberal tradition has produced no great writers, certainly no great recent writers, though Malamud frequently comes close. To a man they make lumpy, misshapen fictions . . . that drone like the lectures Unitarians substitute for sermons, fictions which, in two words, are insufficiently alert. Bad writers in this crowd show the fault most clearly, E. L. Doctorow, for instance."[11]

Gardner concludes, "If we admire the liberals, we admire them more for their goodness than for their art; and too often, as in Doctorow, even the goodness is partly illusory. Saul Bellow is patently and annoyingly a male chauvinist pig. Doctorow lies about history to make his ethically liberal points."[12] Not much contemporary criticism assumes such an assertive tone, and certainly a few, such as Doctorow and Bellow, were likely grateful it didn't. Gardner's tone is a primary reason for his bad boy reputation. If some of the writers aren't as popular as when he wrote about them (or are no longer living), most contemporary writers suffer great degrees of diminishment in comparison. And in this era of correctness of all kinds, Gardner's opinions have the effect of a salutary, mind-clearing antidote.

About the orthodox: "It is Christianity—hellfire Protestant Christianity—not the terrible state of the world, that makes the idea of apocalypse so important in modern American fiction; and it is Christianity of a gentler sort that gives such importance to the idea of resurrection, physical or spiritual."[13] In this category. Gardner, in his unabashed way, places himself, and indeed it was Gardner who popularized and maybe minted the concept of "redemptive" fiction. He includes here Ralph Ellison, Cheever, Gass, Gaddis, Hawkes, Charles Johnson, Pynchon, and in a backhanded way, Robert Coover—"Coover at his worst works exactly like the meanest fundamentalist Baptist."[14]

Then, drawing in Barthelme and John Barth and Gass of *Omensetter's Luck,* Gardner goes a bit further to say, "All of these writers have, in common with Coover, the ex-Christian's love of bathroom humor and fifth-grader irreverence."[15] And he expands on the general outlook of this class of writers by saying that Barth,

> though by nature a cheerful man, talks endlessly, even in his earlier novels, about the meaninglessness of life. No one believes for a moment that he profoundly believes what he says; it's merely fashionable French existentialist bull—; . . . nevertheless he prattles on about suicide and how it makes no difference one way or the other. A pagan Greek would stare in bafflement. "Who cares if life has meaning?" he would say. "Stop nattering and play your flute."[16]

About the diabolists he has little to say, because they aren't, he explains, the engineers of evil they imagine themselves to be—although nowadays he might alter that opinion, considering the fascination with death and vampires and death-dealing as dangerous as a vampire's suck. And the heretics? Perhaps because Gardner was brought up Presbyterian and first wrote sermons, according to his mother, he seems intuitively attuned to the theology of Updike: "And by heretics—my last category—I mean such writers as John Updike, religious men whose ideas of religion I dislike. Updike's message, again and again, is a twisted version of the message of his church, neo-orthodox Presbyterianism: Christ has saved us; nothing is wrong; so come to bed with me."[17]

In a withering review of Walker Percy's *Lancelot* (which was not as withering, however, as I remembered it from 1977, in *The New York Times Book Review*), this is the concluding paragraph:

> Fiction, at its best, is a means of discovery, a philosophical method. By that standard, Walker Percy is not a very good novelist; in fact *Lancelot*, for all its dramatic and philosophical intensity, is bad art, and what's worse, typical bad art. Like Tom Stoppard's plays, it fools around with philosophy, only in this case not for laughs but for fashionable groans. Art, it seems to me, should be a little less pompous, a lot more serious. It should stop sniveling and go for answers or else shut up.[18]

Whether or not you agree with Gardner, his opinions are so strongly and appositely put you're forced to fashion rebuttals, if you can. That is the best way to learn, and this collection is one of the better places to begin. The only American writer who has spoken with anything like Gardner's aptness about contemporaries is John Updike, and Updike's generally milder opinions seem pale in comparison, although some might see Updike's manner as "Christianity of a gentler sort." However that may be, and however these essays strike the thousands they should reach, few will be able to come away from them without a sense of "the man himself." As you hear for the first time or hear again Gardner's voice in these resurrected essays, you realize he remains the figure he always was: a shining light and an enigma.

Gardner's Memorial in Real Time

On the Achievement of Mickelsson

Nabokov has said about Tolstoy, in his Cornell *Lectures on Russian Literature*, that Tolstoy's characters seduce us with their memorable solidity because of "the gift Tolstoy had of endowing his fiction with such time-values as correspond exactly to our sense of time. . . . Tolstoy's prose keeps pace with our pulses, his characters seem to move with the same swing as the people passing under our window while we sit reading the book."[1]

This is not only a precise writerly insight that resounds through our experience of Tolstoy and other excellent fiction, but helps define a standard that's been fluttering noisily overhead for years with heraldry hard to make out through the smoke: Exactly what is good, enduring fiction?

In the vein of Nabokov, I suggest that it's a story in which no sentence can be lifted from its paragraph without doing some violence to the rhythms or the *movement of the story through time*. So it is fiction that contains a clear sense of time—à la Tolstoy—whether to reveal dislocations in time or not, since minute-by-minute time is a universal dimension of reality. This happens to be so because it is reality that fiction settles in or takes off from, no matter what its form or genre. There is no aptness or humor in a departure or, indeed, a departure at all, without the standard of everyday reality as the point to depart from.

In our modern segment of accelerated history we might appear to move at a speed that would cause Tolstoy's nineteenth-century aristocrats (and peasants) to stutter and blink, but there's a speed and limits beyond which the human body will not go. The four-minute mile won't be shaved down to any great degree, for all the concerted efforts; an accomplished Yogi can achieve only limited positions, or contortions, just as an astronaut can withstand only x-amount of gravitational force.

Therefore (you might say), the quickest way to spot an amateur writer is by his or her inaccuracies about the movement of the body through time. This is because each of us has a similar body, with its built-in timepiece, the pulse, the tick-tocker, to refer to. The body is the singular reference that cuts through every cultural and linguistic boundary that the hordes of humanity have constructed over every century since the beginning of time.

Nabokov goes on in his lecture to discuss the two great manipulators of time, Joyce and Proust, and says, "Yet these writers who actually dealt in time values did not do what Tolstoy, quite casually, quite unconsciously does: they move either slower or faster than the reader's grandfather clock; it is the time by Proust or the time by Joyce, not the common average time, a kind of standard time which Tolstoy somehow manages to convey."[2]

It is this exact sense of time, which John Gardner conveys, that serves as a signpost to his accomplishment in *Mickelsson's Ghosts*, his final novel.[3] Average, standard time is so well conveyed it assumes a corporeal dimension—a further character bracketing the bulk of Mickelsson's story. The other indicator of the novel's scope is the richness of Gardner's representation of everyday reality, along with the trembling alterations that reality begins to take on.

When I first encountered *Mickelsson's Ghosts*, in a proof copy the year it appeared, my own sense of reality, which is fairly firm, was displaced for a week, and still is, in a sense, since that week is included in my memory. It was this displacement, rendered in painful exactitude through accumulated detail, that convinced me that *Mickelsson's Ghosts* wasn't a usual novel, or even a better than usual novel, but a novel out of the ordinary.

This perhaps lengthy preface is an attempt to get at the nature of Gardner's achievement in *Mickelsson's Ghosts*—of a grander scope than critics so far have granted. The book, which plumps down with a solid impact merely from the weight of its pages (641 in the uncorrected proofs; 590 when set finer for the finished book) is so encompassing and complex and forthright it seems to elbow its way into a new realm.

It's a novel that few writers could have imagined, in its wit and intellectual content, much less produced, and one reason it has languished for attention, I suspect, is that no critic has been able to fit his or her mind around the disturbing originality of its contours.

It contains dozens of characters of individual heft and dimension, moving through time in a way we recognize, but chiefly Mickelsson, as here:

> He walked cocked forward, as if pitched against a high wind, a largish, stout man in dark, tight trousers and a darker shirt, around his thick neck (if the night was cool) an ascot tie, two fingers clamped tightly on the brim of his hat, holding it down firmly—not really to protect it from gusts, one might have thought, but as if, freed of the pressure of his hat, his head might explode—his steps quick and heavy.[4]

This last whispered breath—"steps quick and heavy"—(nearly as revealing as the lengthy description) works beyond words, due to the accuracy of Gardner's timing within time. As any reader of modern fiction will sense, the attention given to detail in Gardner's description is a further reason for the resistance to *Ghosts*.

Such a reader wouldn't be surprised to find, in a metafictionist's imaginative construct, for instance, a fragmentary scene in which a mermaid on a slope of glass speaks to a shoe about the Cubs. And in the minimal or telegraphic fiction of other mostly "realistic" writers, there is no time for description of this kind—an attitude mocked by Tom McGuane in his novel, *Panama*, when the elegant but somewhat autocratic narrator says, about the agent, Don, who is pursuing him, "I would describe the contents of Don's room but none of it's of any interest."[5]

I doubt this is McGuane's operating aesthetic, considering the rest of his work, but it wryly defines an attitude behind the work of many contemporary writers of fiction. The attitude denies the makeup of a person, or the visible aspects of *some*thing, in the way the order or chaos we view can or cannot hint at a person's or a place's character. The weight of McGuane's insult seems to fall on "describe," because none of this is "of any interest." Not all writers are gifted with a Salingeresque or Joycean gift for detailing the contents of a drawer, for what it might reveal of character, so the contemporary practice is not to describe.

From the narrator's "voice" or from the turns and contours this voice takes on, or in its elisions from the expected, one is to intuit or pick up the necessary elements not just of atmosphere but of setting and character. I'm not exactly sure how a reader is supposed to do this, but every writer has heard arguments for it in university workshops across the United States. The problem is that substance, which is the primary element of life, from this desk to that tree to your body in its present state, ceases to exist. So we have not even an invisible book through which we view the world, as Nabokov reveals in more than one of his novels, but no book and no world beyond, when the method is carried to the extreme.

In *Mickelsson's Ghosts*, the turn is to the opposite, as if to refute the seamless lack of dimension in contemporary fiction. Every scene appears in patient detail, ticking into place with the sound of Nabokov's (or rather Tolstoy's) clock, and our experience of reality is happily confirmed: that it's the most persistent, elusive, diverse, burgeoning, banal, beautiful, frustrating (the modifiers for it fill every dictionary of every language), and common element we daily deal with. It makes up most of our lives and impinges upon them at every point, simply by its ubiquity: material substance overwhelms.

I can't pass through this desk, or that tree or hilltop, or out of my flesh—anyway, not yet. There's no escape from reality, except in certain clinical mental states (most of which are experienced by Mickelsson), in which reality becomes distorted, or is subverted or partially denied—ignored or transformed. I should add that reality is, anyway partly, consensual opinion. As the psychologist Erik H. Erikson puts it in *Gandhi's Truth*, in a statement I often point myself and others to: "'Reality,' of course, is man's most powerful illusion; but while he attends to this world, it must outbalance the total enigma of being in it at all."[6]

No contemporary novel pays greater homage to the endless conjunctions of reality than *Ghosts*. Reality is examined from lofty spiritual and philosophical dimensions down to a pair of stained and callused hands reshaping a portion of reality's basic elements through carpentry. Mickelsson builds. He is fiftyish, a professor and a philosopher whose writings have received "a national reputation," and in the earlier passage he is on one of his nocturnal tours of the university neighborhood where we first meet him.

He's in terrible trouble, of nearly every kind; he's in the midst of a messy divorce and grieving over the separation from a daughter and son. His health is poor, centering on troubles in his stomach and heart; the IRS is after him, he is penurious, at the borderline of insanity once again—he's been treated before—from a corrosive depression he can't break through. And ethics, which has been

Mickelsson's specialty, has been "impatiently snorted away, super-seded by the positive fairytale of 'value-free objectivity.'"[7]

Worse, his "creative juices had dried away to dust."[8] And "the so-called Life of the Mind—of which he'd once written so glowingly"[9]—has driven him so entirely into his own mind, where shadows of himself and others echo and collide, that his mind has become a portable hell.

He sits in a sweltering room, "the narrow space his life's errors had left him,"[10] trying to force himself to write under a searing desk lamp, or stares at "some wretched girlie mag, strangling the goose."[11] It should be apparent by now that the locutions are Mickelsson's, not Gardner's, and that they reveal character in the most succinct and artful way—through the texture of a character's language, here tuned to a rural Wisconsinite of Mickelsson's age.

This use of language is different from the earlier method mentioned, which supposedly implies, sometimes merely through the topography of prose, rudimentary elements of character and setting. Why should a writer be concerned with place? As surely as a plant won't grow without soil, or even a fake substitute for soil, so no fictional character of any stature has risen, or will rise, from a vacuum. Place is the foundation of fiction.

Even the most rudimentary descriptions in this novel take on not only the timing but the rumble and the tinge of a particular voice:

> Mickelsson, once the most ordinary of men, a philosopher almost obsessively devoted to precision and neatness (despite his love of Nietzsche), distrustful if not downright disdainful of passion (his pencils always sharpened and formally lined up, from longest to shortest, even in his pocket), a man dispositionally the product of a long line of Lutheran ministers and one incongruous, inarticu-lately rebellious dairy farmer, Mickelsson's father . . . [Gardner's ellipsis.] Who would have thought that he, Peter Mickelsson, could come to this? Sweating, drinking, listening for visitors, sleeping off depressions and hangovers, he wasted so much time (more and more, these days) he began to feel almost constant guilt and panic.[12]

These descriptions accumulate until we enter Mickelsson's person, and our chronological sense slows to the fussy and farmerish sense of time under his educated exterior—peering out, as it were, over the threshold of his mind. Few contemporary novels are as painstakingly built from the bottom up.

The visitors he mentions are students and young colleagues from the university, and for anyone to whom the life of the mind is as important as it is to Mickelsson, unwanted visitors or personal involvement in the troubles of others (as exemplified by the student, Nugent) only bring disorder. Several lengthy and well-drawn scenes of two of Mickelsson's classes illustrate this, and in those instances Mickelsson is always striving (with more insistence and art than many university professors, I might add) to bring balance and order to each classroom session. The proper balance would, of course, represent his internal equipoise. He's being invaded, he realizes, and the invasion is altering him.

In his first interview with Nugent, a student who is supposedly suicidal and has been foisted on him by the head of the philosophy department, Mickelsson finds himself thinking, "What a world . . . shepherding another poor innocent . . . into the treacherous, ego-bloated, murder-stained hovel of philosophy."[13] What a way to view philosophy, or to describe his own métier! Mickelsson's response to the interview? He immediately decides to buy a house in the country. He can't afford such a place, he knows, yet his search becomes obsessive. He considers the possibility of being "in the possession of some demon, that is, some daemonic idea."[14] The corrective measure in his definition is relevant; as a philosopher or plain intellectual, he can't tolerate the idea of being possessed.

He begins to carry on conversations, both real and imaginary (he has a habit of talking to himself, gesturing close to his chest), with his psychiatrist and his lawyer about his reasons for buying a house in the country. He decides to use as down payment money he's been putting aside in case "his mother should need a nursing home."[15]

He has earlier sensed that some of his justifications about himself are "beginning to sound like Heidegger in the days of the Führer," and as he deals with dishonest real estate agents he discovers he is developing an amazing ability to lie.[16] About the lying, he thinks:

> An existentialist, of course, could defend it without a blink; another kind of thinker could argue its rightness in a community of liars; another might assert its suitability to a stock behavioral mode voluntarily elected; but Mickelsson . . . had never been friendly to the notion that human beings are free to turn into tomato plants at will, or even to the best utilitarianism, and least of all to R. M. Hare's opinion, Oxonian and therefore unassailable, that morality is life-style.[17]

Thought itself, often disconnected except to other thought, occupies Mickelsson almost entirely, and Gardner's purpose soon becomes clear: if the life of the mind is to anyone real life, and that life is organized around the scruples mentioned above, then to act and live at variance with those scruples, or to drift through situations engaged in numbing thought, is to invite worse disorder than outside invasion, or possession, might bring. To live and act in this way is indeed to alter life, or change the cast of reality for oneself, and *Mickelsson's Ghosts* is about a man who finds he is forgoing the gospel that formed his character.

His downward slide into relative values, with fewer attachments to reality, picks up speed when he finds the house. Four full pages are spent describing his first impression of it, with not many wasted words. A nearly "ungraspable phantom meaning"[18] comes over him and at the end of his kaleidoscopic impression he thinks: "Here stood this house, possibility of escape—increasingly sombre in the deepening twilight—and there, all around it, to his imagination, were the stretched-out bony arms of those with legitimate demands. He forgot what he'd been thinking."[19]

Reality has slipped from him. For the moment he can't even retain consecutive thought, and the next chapter of the book ends: "He seemed to have lost the ability to tell the truth."[20] He has left his former life behind, and now the house becomes his life. He holds "Open House," as in the Roethke poem of that title—a bearish, diffident, vulnerable man like Roethke, the doors of his mind flung wide to every floating influence—and the house stands as a pictorial representation of his mental state. He will remake it according to his will, he believes. Many of the most revealing scenes in the novel capture this remaking, as Mickelsson engages hard-edged reality through carpentry, his mind soaring free.

The "Ghosts" of the title are those shadows and echoes of others and his earlier self that Mickelsson is continually entangled with, as surely as they are the ghosts that begin to appear in the house. There are hundreds of philosophical and sociohistorical and political echoes, along with a lapful of literary ones, but Nietzsche and Luther are the towering figures, the antipodes, that Mickelsson stands between and pits himself against. He achieves a rapport and measuring stance with that historic duo—no mean feat in itself. Both embody aspects of Mickelsson, and the trio carries forward the major themes of this immensely architectonic novel: grace, self-willed superhumanism, and the creativity whose pulse and roots are in realism. Nature is as large a force as any figure.

Mickelsson also directly confronts God, and sometimes prays to him, while, at the other end of the spectrum, he tries to evade the cold hand of a materialized ghost on his arm. And in the midst of the actual, or somewhere in between, he deals with the house and the mechanical problems of his ancient vehicles and finally with a heavy-breathing assassin who holds a pistol on him. As Mickelsson becomes more unmoored, drifting into the "value-free objectivity" he detests, a boundless fury, awesome in its all-inclusiveness, seethes: "As Luther had hated the long dark shadow of the Pope, and as Nietzsche had hated Luther, Mickelsson hated everything, everybody, every remotest possibility. He hated works, he hated grace, he hated the retreat to love in all its permutations."[21]

This fury, sealed over by his depression, takes on the form of a languid passiveness, the calm of a cold-blooded killer. Mickelsson does kill a dog, at the very minimum, and perhaps a person; and the outgrowth of certain of his actions may be responsible for other deaths. I say "may" and "perhaps," because the reader comes to realize that the central tension of this huge and ambitious book, and its grappling hook at one's heart (it can be that rough), is its questioning of our premises of what is real, or what reality is, once the reality we perceive in general has been so precisely and painstakingly set in place to the tick of that universal clock. In its examination of the borderlines of reality, and of borderline states of mental illness and health, it becomes the kind of book that can alter one's way of perceiving the world.

Once Mickelsson has escaped the university town, Binghamton, New York—one of the many carefully rendered settings of the novel—and moved to the farmhouse in neighboring Pennsylvania, his unsettling encounters with reality begin. Inexplicable sensations and dreams invade him, containing telltale links to details in the house. It has been suggested to Mickelsson by a banker and a real estate agent, besides a rural neighbor, Pearson, that the house is haunted, and soon a pair of ghosts appears—an elderly couple as solid as the front door, from which Mickelsson cut away a hex sign when he moved in.

Strange smells rise in the house. Mysterious seepages appear on the land bordering it. Semitrailers with their lights off barrel down Mickelsson's backwoods road late at night. Most of this baffles Mickelsson, when it doesn't terrify him, but he's soon buried again in the examination of his own shortcomings and problems, turning the outside world inward. These examinations grow increasingly searching while his ability to do anything about himself and his besetting sins fades to faint mists. Ghosts. He bats away certain thoughts as if shooing flies as he works on the house.

His rage shifts him into a perspective from which he launches one of the most excoriating attacks on the sixties and seventies in print—a glacial negation in the line of Nietzsche. He serves as unconscious matchmaker in a romance between Brenda Winburn, a student he pinpoints as the nihilist of one class, and Alan Blassenheim, the moral idealist, in a need to marry some of the disorder in himself. When he discovers that Brenda is actually in love with him, he is able to treat her like his actual daughter, who later appears in a few scattered but moving scenes.

Tim Booker, the realtor who has shown Mickelsson the house, is actually a Hells Angel, or a witch, as the neighbor Pearson turns out to be—in Booker's case a "white witch," to use a contemporary term, considering the book's denouement. Booker is also a pimp. He introduces Mickelsson to Donnie Matthews, a teenage prostitute who entraps Mickelsson and tempts him to rob the "fat man" who apparently dies of a heart attack at the shock of Mickelsson's break-in. A murder of the heart.

The gracious woman physician from whom Mickelsson has bought the house is charged with malpractice by a neighbor who claims he can fly; he claims she's a murderess. And she does nearly run down Mickelsson with her car one winter night when she's supposed to be in Florida. If any of this sounds the least bit whimsical (not the most congenial mode in Gardner), it is not; it's realistic fiction of the most spellbinding sort, striding ahead like the strokes of one's pulse, and then taking sudden breathless leaps into the dark holes in space that most novelists shy from.

The house Mickelsson has moved to once was, as it turns out, a residence of Joseph Smith, the founder of Mormonism, and the Mormons—actual visiting church members and a wing of assassins, the Sons of Dan—now get hold of Mickelsson. Donnie Matthews already has him in her grip; Mickelsson is obsessive about his involvement with her. The IRS visits and fastens its talons. And a grip of another kind is gained by Owen Thomas, the owner of the local hardware store where Mickelsson charges tools and supplies for remodeling his house—the grip of financial indebtedness, adding to Mickelsson's already unpaid debts, but indebtedness, too, of a psychic kind. Thomas is the kind of person who calmly, even kindly, entices Mickelsson to get in deeper.

And overarching all of these is Jessica Stark, a newly widowed colleague in the Sociology Department at Binghamton. She seems to Mickelsson too beautiful and imposing to consider; she's also Jewish, a "first-class scholar" with a "rabbinical wit."[22] During a wonderfully orchestrated all-night conversation with her, Mickelsson notes of her densely freckled skin that it is "unearthly but beautiful, as if she were a figure built up of precious metals and then transformed, imperfectly, into an ordinary mortal. Her freckles were buried level after level, like stars in the Milky Way: she was a thousand colors, like some dense impressionistic painting."[23]

Jessica Stark, or Jessie, as Mickelsson calls her, is a creature whose reality is uncertain, although her density is clear. She is made up of contradictory layers and is as difficult to understand at times as a best friend or spouse. Her eventual union with Mickelsson, most notably at the book's conclusion, draws many pointillist subthemes of the novel into the major chromatic scale of depiction in Mickelsson.

She has lost not only her husband but two daughters, and the depth of her loss renders her substantial in a way that Donnie, who claims to be carrying Mickelsson's child, will never be. In Donnie's apartment, Mickelsson sees that, "In the crisp morning light, the cracked paint on the window sash was like writing, like some form of Arabic."[24] And then, turning to Donnie: "He looked at the pattern of veins in her chest and thought—not quite seriously but seriously playing with the possibility—that at any instant . . . she too would be language, all mysteries revealed."[25]

It would be simplistic to say, though not beyond the pale, that she can be easily read. She inspires him to begin, rather foolishly, a "blockbuster of a book" on philosophy that he is never able to finish. Here, as at other junctures, the tone turns a bit pompous, or academic, with here and there a feeling of being constructed rather than unfolding in front of us like cinematic scenes, as in the best of this novel, the authorial hand absent.

A beauty-and-the-beast theme runs through the center of the novel's multiple meanings. Jessica is attracted to Mickelsson, if not in love with him, and they spend profoundly idyllic and sexual inter-ludes together. In a tightening variation, she is attracted to Tillson, too, the head of the Philosophy Department, a hunchbacked, goat-eyed pragmatist attuned to every wind of change—the perfect administrator.

When Tillson sees a month-old pile of mail that Mickelsson, in his deepening depression, has allowed to accumulate in his office, Tillson asks if such neglect is "ethical." Mickelsson is not permit-ted to escape the person and philosopher he was. Tillson and the dean of Mickelsson's college, Sheldon Blickstein, are two of the substantial "ghosts"—both with unusual physical shapes, both patchily educated—who begin closing in on Mickelsson's life at his country house.

By now he is entirely revamping the place, and also beginning to bear down in his classes. He reveals, in a medical ethics seminar, that he is opposed to abortion, although not strongly enough to keep from upsetting a Polish woman who is a refraction of Jessica. But when Donnie, who has inexplicably traveled to California, tells him she is pregnant by him, he agrees she should have an abortion and pays for it. His growing ambivalence to life and death, or death-in-life (the "child-angel" in him is in anguish at the sudden onslaught of age), is dramatized in other classroom encounters—some of the best you'll find in fiction—where the lives and deaths of minds, yes, but also actual physical lives, too, hang in the balance.

Nugent is discovered with his throat slit, an apparent suicide, but has likely been murdered because of his involvement with a gay group, one of whose members was gathering the goods on the Sons of Dan. The spiritual deadness of some of the cults that derive from Christianity and some of the deadness of Christianity itself (largely through the figure of Luther) are examined. Also present are counter-themes on ecology, nuclear weapons, UFOs, and the interpenetration of other forms of life into this one, the student underground, and the deadly underworld.

We encounter looping referrals to Mickelsson's former psychiatrist, Rifkin, and discussions with him of the "Great Cryptogram."[26] Then another ghost, a boy, appears at the house, and Mickelsson sees "the present lining up with the past, like one image superimposed on the other."[27] Mickelsson senses, in his "reading into" everything at this point, that the landscape is about to spell a message, or a barbed wire fence a syllogism (from Wittgenstein, of course), and once, at his rural mailbox, it seems the thunder is God clearing his throat before he speaks—we feel that close to an event of infinite consequence.

If you're beginning to suffer the impression that Mickelsson ("mickle" means "great" or "much") might be taking on the entire world, then attend: "He'd become once more the suicidal Dadaist, representative hero and symbol of his nation—perhaps the secret center of all men and nations—fallen out of orbit, drifting like his civilization toward catastrophe."[28] This reverberates not only with Milton but a description Jesus gives to his apostles: "I saw Satan fall like lightning from heaven."

Besides the novel's unveiling of everyday reality, it examines the illusions and the reality of Satanism, demonology, witchcraft, philosophy, religion, education, community, and nearly every organization and force that derive from reality. The point it makes as a whole, as it tests our ability to survive in differing degrees of reality (or our illusions of "reality"), is that we operate more than we realize, or would like to admit, at the mercy of forces beyond our control.

These forces are particularized by the "falls" that a colleague who teaches history, Freddy Rogers, discusses with Mickelsson—"frogs falling out of the sky, or blood, or fish . . . cookies in unmarked plastic bags." Rogers forges on: "I saw the fall of little stones out in Chico, California—maybe you read about it; it made a lot of papers . . . 'Right out of the clear blue sky,' as the saying goes . . . We just stood there with our hands folded and looked. Even in Chico nobody believed it except the people who were right there and saw it."[29] (Gardner taught for some years at Chico State).

Reality is not only everywhere and everything, Gardner is saying, but reality is at best imperfectly explained. *Mickelsson's Ghosts* is above all a cautionary tale, and it should be read that way, as a warning to students and professors who feel they can remain unaffected by the genial and "objective," value-free atmosphere of a university—without gradually giving over their first love until it's a ghost of what it once was, then is gone.

If some readers would like to know more about Jessica's work in sociology, or about the daughters she has lost, then it's also true that when you explain away one mystery, you only make room for another, as the writer and editor William Maxwell has observed. A novelist doesn't deal in explanations, but acts.

Gardner could have resolved more questions about Jessica in a few sentences, if he'd wished, considering the complexities he does resolve. That he chooses not to adds to his view of reality's imperfection. If we wonder why such a lengthy section of the book is devoted to a visit by Mickelsson to the Adirondacks, when nothing overt happens, then we're reminded that this is the way of most of reality; and that Mickelsson once lived a similar life in the midst of nature, in Wisconsin, in those scenes in which he places himself and his family.

And if his languid passiveness or slowed and patient deliberations sometimes tempt us to say, "Come on, Mickelsson, call Jessica," or "Please, Mickelsson, DO something," it's because we're involved in what Mickelsson is doing or not doing.

Some might question the spacious elaborations on the Swissons, a young couple in music, whose recital Mickelsson and Jessica attend. At first Mickelsson sees the married couple as "twins," and the husband's darkly rotted teeth are like the teeth of Jessica's husband, as he appears at the close of the novel, just as Kate Swisson's gangling gracelessness is like the gracelessness of the female physician from whom Mickelsson bought the house—in this novel in which every character has a further ghost or doppelganger.

The Swissons underscore the Nordic, tragicomic, operatic strain in Mickelsson, along with the twinning and triplication that is his essence. It is through the Swissons that Mickelsson embarks upon one of the major meditations of the novel—on the makeup of music and its aesthetic. This takes on the allusive and swelling intricacy of thought that's possible only when you're working at something else, as Mickelsson is when the meditation begins. Finally, as he listens with "strained intensity" to a piece of music, he thinks: "Wasn't it the case, in fact, that he'd been listening all this while for the wrong thing entirely; that music—for that matter, all the arts—told one nothing at all, simply described things as they are, or were, or might be, simply named things as Adam was said to have named things in the garden except that it was the thing named?"[30]

This is the central aesthetic of *Mickelsson's Ghosts*, and its central meaning: the things of this world as they are, nailed by naming. It is during this meditation, as essential to the novel as Nabokov's meditation on time in *Ada*, when Mickelsson's mind reaches toward the music of the spheres he has alluded to, that the reader comes to understand Gardner's careful consideration of the timing within time that is this novel's outstanding attribute.

It is written with the same ear for time that the notations of music take across its lines and staves. And it's clear from this that Gardner has studied music, was a student of music—a French horn player.

If some of the meditations and discussions in the novel appear set up or patted along, to press the action of the book forward, at least it keeps moving, for its bulk, within the stately progression of foursquare time. Great chords of harmony are struck forward and back over the themes and subthemes, and the more carefully you read or reread, the more each detail is subsumed within the story's symphonic structure. If the prose isn't always in the poetic strain of a younger Gardner, a prose so brightly observant it has the aspect of ripe wheat under summer sun (see *Nickel Mountain*, and the later sections of *October Light*), then this is an older person's darker story, darkly tuned to the erosions of age and the cadences of Mickelsson's love: rhetoric.

Or, as Mickelsson says of his philosophy, "if he was occasionally careless, at times drawn too far by his love for rhetoric and inclination to shock, he was nonetheless a better philosopher—bolder and more original—than a vast majority of the nit-picking dullards one encountered in the so-called discipline these days."[31]

Most of the novel is in Gardner's straightforward, meaty prose, which makes no more nor less of itself than it is and can assume a resonant strength, with the bulking aura in it of a body's breathing heat. More than perhaps any contemporary, Gardner transmits a tactile presence. The book's three parts form a shapely urn, the first and last parts nearly equal, the center thicker by a section, mirroring Mickelsson's physical shape, and his tippable, suggestible character.

The architectonic strands of the story are always clear, considering the number and complexity of them and the breadth of distance they sometimes have to span to complete their weave. The boxes within boxes of interleaved material open in the proper order, down to the boxes Mickelsson begins to build, in a comically manic phase, within the box of the house he is rebuilding, until he comes across the central box that everybody in the book is after, including the assassin with the pistol. I refuse to spill the brilliant contents of the least of these for the slothful reader, or to diminish the joy of discovery for the reader who perseveres.

As Mickelsson rebuilds the house in the form of himself, it's as if he begins to arrive, experientially, where his philosophy began.

He sees through Jessie the possibility, "the strange assumption—or faith, rather—that even quite terrible evils, betrayals, mistakes might be forgiven."[32] And when a faculty member (also a member of the Sons of Dan?) holds a pistol on him and forces him to tear apart the entire house and Mickelsson sends out a final, psychic cry for help, it arrives from both the ghostly otherworld and the actual world of neighborhood people he knows.

It arrives in differing ways and in larger numbers than Mickelsson could have imagined. The arcs of his giants, Luther and Nietzsche, finally intersect, as he recalls how Nietzsche,

> in his final great madness, abased himself, throwing himself down, to no avail, before Cosima Wagner, admitting at last, symbolically, however futilely, the necessity of what he'd dismissed from his system, amazing grace; whereas Luther remained to the end righteous and stiff-necked, for all his rhetorical self-abasement—remained, in Mickelsson's grandfather's phrase, a sinner besmirched beyond all washing but the Lord's.[33]

So it is that Mickelsson abases himself before Jessie. His son Mark, who has been absent for the entire novel, involved in the anti-nuclear underground (or else a perfect corporeal projection of Mark supplied in Mickelsson's need), appears on a couch in the torn-apart house, asleep—a forgiven presence reappearing. Mickelsson's head by now has exploded (as in the Dylan song, "The Locusts Sang," also about academia), or imploded; there is no more division between reality and the world imagined. Before Mickelsson leaves to see Jessica, he dresses in a costume, at least part of which—a red hunting jacket—is a match to the cap of that other outcast and social critic, Holden Caulfield.

Leaving Holden's generational equivalent asleep on the couch, Mickelsson goes off to give voice to a mature man's protests, emptied of intellectual pretense, a shattered hulk of his former self, a ghost.

With a flutter of horror the reader wonders whether the detailed representation of the reality of this six-hundred-and-some-page book hasn't turned its author, John Gardner—clearly an analogue of Mickelsson—inside out. The ghostly characters of the novel Mickelsson encounters at Jessica's seem to say that for all the substantiality we might picture or sense from characters in fiction (even those of the most memorable solidity, as in this novel), they are ultimately creatures of the creator's imagination—ghosts.

Even their ghost shapes are coming apart molecularly, as Jessica was first seen as built up in glowing layers of color and disarray. And when a further swarm of ghosts gathers around the bed to witness the final union of Mickelsson and Jessie "both people and animals, an occasional bird, still more beyond, some of them laughing, some looking away (Mormons, Presbyterians), some blowing their noses and brushing away tears . . . ,"[34] what we notice is their fearful clamoring to be born, to be involved with reality, to be living, in contrast to most people's lack of gratitude for life.

Meanwhile bones are tumbling onto the lawn, blood is falling and boiling as it hits outside the window in this last great conjunction of illusion and reality and commingling of it, while the rest of the scenes in the book begin to fall, solid as stones, backward into the places they were intended to occupy.

Whether Gardner purposely wrote a good-bye to his readers or to the reality of the world we contend with daily, or whether he planned to burrow as far as he could into the implications of reality before he bid his readers good-bye, I don't see how he could have done better than in this most ambitious of his novels, the one that will come to stand, when every mode of reassessment is finished, as the most substantial of his achievements, *Mickelsson's Ghosts*.

6

GOSPELS OF REYNOLDS PRICE

On Trials of Translating

Running tandem if not abreast with the luminous literary works of Reynolds Price is his abiding interest in the Bible. He not only leans his stories on the stories he has encountered in the Bible but also has attempted in a variety of ways to penetrate the mystery of Scripture's appeal. His pilgrimage perhaps began when he learned Koine Greek (the *lingua franca* of the Gospels, in contrast to the classical literary Greek of Homer) and rendered his first translation of Mark twenty-five years ago, in *A Palpable God*.

His recent book, *Three Gospels*, contains an updated version of Mark, a new translation of John, and "An Honest Account of a Memorable Life: An Apocryphal Gospel."[1] The last is Price's own, strung along the bones of Mark's narrative, with portions of other accounts included—all informed by Price's reading in historical and scholarly and theological sources, beside his firsthand experience of the weather and geography of Palestine. It was in Palestine, in a vision, that Price was healed of the worst effects of the spinal cancer that should have done him in through a manifestation of the presence of Jesus, as he details in his earlier memoir, *A Whole New Life: An Illness and a Healing*.

This gospel is also an assignment, the result of a seminar Price conducted on the Gospels, in which each member composed a narrative of his or her own, and Price fulfilled his own assignment: "The simplest justification for the effort, and one that has lain behind the thousands of attempts on Jesus that have burdened libraries for the past two millennia, is that the career of a particular Palestinian Jew of the first century and the effects of that life on world history have proved so magnetic in their mystery as to demand ceaseless watch and question. . . ."[2]

An enduring beauty of Price's book is its ability to view the Gospel narratives as stories encountered for the first time. His prefaces to each are excellent. In fact, if anyone wanted an introduction to the Gospels, or wondered why they should have one, they might turn first to Price's book, rather than a contemporary theologian. They are that good, tempering a breadth of scholarly study with Price's good sense as an intuitive storyteller.

He laments the state of present Bible scholarship, even translating the Bible's usual "scribes and Pharisees" as "*scholars* and Pharisees." In acknowledging some of his sources, he says he is especially indebted to "those studies by the almost unimaginably well-prepared scholars of the late nineteenth and early twentieth centuries before the mainstream of German, British, and American scholarship succumbed to its present obsession with a punitively unreasonable degree of historical doubt."[3]

Doubt to this degree does not prevail, as he points out, in literary scholarship. The earliest papyri of Homer's *Iliad*, for example, date from at least 500 years after its composition, and all the fragments and variations number 643. Greek manuscripts of the New Testament number over five thousand, and the number keeps growing, including papyrus fragments of Matthew, discovered in 1995, which were dated to the middle of the first century, the era of its composition—further proof that early compilers of the Greek New Testament were accurate in placing the Gospel of Matthew first. If copies of the New Testament translated into Latin and Syriac and Ethiopic and Slavic and other languages from the second and third centuries are added to this total (two to three centuries closer than the fragments of Homer), the number escalates to over twenty-four thousand. In none of this number are there any disquieting variants from text to text.

It's wise to keep this in mind when considering the inordinate attention given to the Gnostic writings and the present day scholarship expended on these and the Gospels of Thomas and Judas and similar ephemeral artifacts. Those who attend to Scripture or refer to it are often called, in the modern form of politically correct dismissal, fundamentalists. Fundamentalism of a Christian sort, and not other varieties, is belabored as a besetting evil in a sameness of voice that Christian fundamentalists are supposed to have, when most branches of fundamentalism are involved in continual arguments with, if not in opposition to, a dozen other branches.

Fundamentalism, the word, with no knowledge of its origin, is the *bête noire* of intellectuals who seem to have fallen prey, as Solzhenitsyn predicted, to the idea that they are governing gods accountable to no one, ill-mannered in their self-centeredness, urged on by the ill-mannered Lilliputians on their TV screens who promote a one-dimensional view—the leveling agent of Big Brother, with sound bites of newspeak, just as Orwell warned.

A shift may be in the works, however, because an honest intellectual recently noted that a general consensus is that "fundamentalist Christians tend to be somewhat intolerant of nonbelievers. But as the author of *Biographia Literaria* knew, there are truths that 'are too often considered as *so* true, that they lose all the life and efficiency of truth, and lie bed-ridden in the dormitory of the soul, side by side with the most despised and exploded errors.'"[4] The dormitory image from Coleridge, as quoted by Michael Robbins in the December 2008 issue of *Poetry*, is especially applicable to the sophomoric attitude of intellectuals who are not "somewhat intolerant" but are abusive in their speech and attitude toward "fundamentalist Christians."

I recently received a Thanksgiving message from a college

professor in which he listed many reasons to be thankful, but was "realistic" about other matters that remained unresolved, and ended with, "so not everything is Good News, as Christian fundamentalists would have us believe." The professor is the author of a book that excoriates a modern writer for the anti-Semitism in his work, and apparently doesn't realize he's fallen into the same error toward the other side, in his wholesale dismissal.

This dismissal is the flat-line sameness repeated by almost every professor in every university, where the uni-mind sets aside diversity. How do they dismiss twenty centuries of literature built on the basis of a fundamental belief in the Bible? The TV prognosticators, attended to with the avidity once reserved for the prophets of Scripture, have won. The flat-line numbness is penetrating even Christians who aspire to intellectual credibility. I lately heard a person who calls himself an open-minded Christian, one who should know better, say, "Evangelicals are just Christian fundamentalists in disguise."

This would dismiss believers such as Bonhoeffer and Barth. The sad truth is that Christianity is being removed from education and the marketplace, anywhere where it might attain traction, as systematically as it was removed from the Protestant churches in Germany when Hitler rose to power, replaced by Aryan worship and mindlessness.

Price deletes the most substantial extant variant from his gospel of Mark—its final eleven, summary verses, which do not appear in some of the earliest manuscripts. He has a storyteller's concerns and a translator's conscience. Some modern translators' attempts to find a "dynamic equivalence" for first-century Greek "are logically suspect in the extreme," he writes, "but have been pursued so often by individuals and groups that now we have in English several popular versions of the gospels that constitute what are well-intended but almost certainly major distortions of their originals."[5]

This clear-eyed view should cause readers of Price to sit up straight, as his translations do. He views Mark, who was anciently known as "stump-fingered," not as the possessor of short, thick fingers but all thumbs with language. His eloquence, Price suggests, "rises from the struggle between Mark's headlong intent and his gravely hobbled command of his medium"—a Galilean Jew using Greek.[6] Here is Price's rendering of one well-known portion: "John wore camel's hair and a leather belt round his hips, ate grasshoppers and wild honey and declared 'He's coming who is stronger than I— after me—of whom I'm unfit stooping to loosen the strap of his sandals. I baptized you in water but he'll baptize you in Holy Spirit.'"[7]

Three Gospels, falling near the apex of Price's career, is a wonderfully engrossing book. It moves with a care and lucidity that should offend few (though it's bound to get the goat of the fringe, both fundamentalist and liberal) and should provide a new perspective for many. "If veteran readers of John can make the effort to approach his gospel freshly," Price writes, ". . . they may begin to see what atheists and agnostics will sight at once—the hair-raising newness of one slender tract."[8]

Glimpses of that newness from a seasoned storyteller's perspective render the *Three Gospels* especially attractive, along with the hundreds of observations Price scatters along the way from the practical wisdom he's accumulated over decades of carefully written essays, short stories, novellas, and novels. The book brims with mature and seasoned assessment, with unconcealed concern and warmth, and reveals the affinities to the Bible's narratives that often underlie (however unspoken) a continued literary production of the nature and stature present in the work of Reynolds Price.

Updike's Sheltered Self

On America's Maestro

I

A stellar panorama over contemporary literature went down with the death of John Updike. I was shocked and angered (that he would do this!), and then disconcerted, unable to sleep—the central cause of my upset that a book or two would not descend every year, as they had for the past fifty from a kind of literary heaven, always with artful and engaging (indeed, sometimes shocking) passages, along with a new outlook and slant, in the latest addition to an oeuvre that was protean and distinguished and, no matter which direction it took, Updikean.

No writer has added to the direction of letters in the latter half of the twentieth century, in America and across the globe, quite like Updike, not only through his fiction but by directing readers to writers of distinction from other countries and cultures in his essays and reviews. He was canny and witty but not the sort who sought the public eye by outrageous behavior or catty remarks on TV (at a time when writers actually appeared on talk shows), nor an absentee who toyed with his material in a way that caused the reader to wonder about its personal reference, and his shapely fictions didn't devolve into philosophical asides or conundrums, as with some—he saved those for his essays. The only comparisons to his silken and often seamless prose, though no comparison really quite fits, are Henry James and James Joyce and Marcel Proust, with a dash of Henry Green. It is that good.

From the first his work conveyed the feel of a professional, with the onrush of one who has found and knows his voice, along with a touching and friendly elderly fussiness about accuracy. His first novel, indeed, was about elderly men in an old folks' home. The central character, Hook, based on a memorable character from Updike's early autobiographical stories, his maternal grandfather, John Hoyer, as Updike has mentioned in essays and autobiographical asides, was a hook to an earlier age that Updike, though he could be adventuresome and innovative, never quite left.

In the week I heard of his death, I was looking over a long essay I once wrote on his work, and then added to and rewrote—an essay he said he had seen on one of the few occasions we met, and then smiled. It was a mild, ruminative smile, not one to put me down, and reminded me of his gracious nature in our few encounters and exchanges of letters and phone conversations. I don't feel I will cause him unrest, therefore, to revisit the essay, which I've revised once more; and if it seems to contain too many versions of the phrase he often encountered, "Yes, but . . ." as I reassess a contemporary whose work I admire above most others, the diligent auditor will note that nearly all the *buts* relate to the same point: Updike's professed Christianity measured against the content of his work.

In the spring of 1964, when I was twenty-two and living in a rented room in New York City, I read my first Updike novel, *The Centaur*. The setting of my reading was seedy and unromantic—a room on St. Mark's Place, before St. Mark's became fashionable, that rented for nine dollars a week, but I can, à la Proust, recapture the dimensional sparkle that rose from the objects of that dingy room as I descended into Updike's prose. No modern writer I had read before generated quite that effect.

I returned to his earlier books and caught up, not such a difficult task at the time, just as *The Olinger Stories*, bound together like a packet of love letters, as Updike's preface put it, appeared. I knew the stories, so I read the preface standing in the Eighth Street bookstore in shoes worn so thin from walking I could feel the texture of city sidewalks through my socks.

In 1965, the year I was married, *Assorted Prose* and *Of The Farm* appeared, and in 1968, when our first daughter was born, *Couples* started climbing the bestseller list. I could date the appearance of every Updike book I've read, approximately fifty, in relationship to my life, but rather than advance myself as a candidate for another exiguous and uxorious (Updike words) recounting as in Nicholson Baker's *U and I*, I want to pause at this pair of novels, *Of The Farm* and *Couples*, because they represent a watershed in Updike's career.

I agree that *Of The Farm* was, as the critic Peter Buitenhuis said in *The New York Times Book Review* when the novel appeared, "very clearly and very completely, a small masterpiece."[1] But I also found it depressing, a new response for me to Updike. The exhilarating sparkle that had the power to transform the mundane seemed to withdraw whenever I looked up from *Of The Farm*, and I sensed a troubling darkness.

Perhaps it was the subject matter, I decided. I was newly married and had only half a heart to follow three generations of a family (the "quartet of voices" that Updike's self-composed flap copy describes) try to resettle themselves in emotionally convoluted ways around a recent divorce. The seriocomic edge of Updike's most spacious and winning character, George Caldwell, and every Updike variation on Caldwell, was absent—he had died offstage. As *Of The Farm* circled the several stories of betrayal at its center—mother of father, Joey of his first wife, mother and Joey of aspects of that wife, mother of Joey's present wife—I, too, felt betrayed. The emotional omnivorousness of Joey's mother, Mrs. Robinson ("Hey, Mrs. Robinson!" Simon and Garfunkel were soon to sing), did not seem, in the fictional context, a credible cause for the divorce, but chosen for the engine of the novel, which might well have been called *Joey's Choice*: pragmatism.

In retrospect, I find *Of The Farm* among Updike's most artful novels, its compression alone a poetic feat—scarcely a wasted action in 150 pages—and it's the novel I would recommend when people wonder where to start in Updike. The original cloth version from Knopf runs to 173 pages, but each page won't quite fill a regular, double-spaced typed page—a book designer's artful construct: causing a novella to assume at least partially a novel's heft. The Ballantine paperback is 129 pages.

Here and there in *Of The Farm*, one runs into patches of highly stylized prose, as critics of the day noted, when Updike's accent becomes rather too canted toward the literary, as here, when the recent divorcé, Joey, is mowing his mother's rural meadow with a small, Fordson-style tractor:

> Crickets sprang crackling away from the wheels; butterflies loped [sic] through their tumbling universe and bobbed above the flattened grass as the hands of a mute concubine would examine, flutteringly, the corpse of her giant lover. The sun grew higher. The metal hood acquired a nimbus of heat waves that visually warped each stalk. The tractor body was flecked with foam and I, rocked back and forth on the iron seat shaped like a woman's hips, alone in nature, as hidden under the glaring sky as at midnight, excited by destruction, weightless, discovered in myself a swelling which I idly permitted to stand, thinking of Peggy.[2]

Peggy is Joey's new wife, and it is those hands of a mute concubine examining a corpse that begin to warp not every word, as the nimbus of heat would not warp *each* stalk, but enough of them so that "the tractor body flecked with foam" (inaccurate, while adverbs keep flying, plus the poised "weightless" a mature Updike would shun), renders the swelling "in" Joey—surely not inside him—which is "idly permitted to stand," comic. One isn't entirely sure if the overplay is intended to be comic or ironic. The flex and outpour of the passage, however, is unmistakable; the reader is in the presence of an authentic poetic voice of individuality and power.

The response of critics to such passages, not only in *Of The Farm* but other early Updike, was so brutal on occasion it left me, a mere bystander, stunned. In *Esquire*, the middle-aged Norman Mailer, surveying the field of rising young writers for any with the potential to eclipse him (in "Some Children of the Goddess"), summarily dismissed the opening and closing paragraphs of *Rabbit, Run*, the most telling passages of any novel, and went on to say that the book contained "one thousand other imprecise, flatulent, wry-necked, precious, overpreened, self-indulgent, tortured sentences."[3]

John Aldridge, in a review so cruel I came away with the impression he wanted Updike dead, commanded him to shut up, since he had nothing to say. Leslie Fiedler called him "strangely irrelevant." Although Updike was publishing almost weekly in the *New Yorker*, in one department or another, his early fiction did not find favor with the New York literati, to such a degree that he became (perhaps on the basis of no more than the homophone of his initials, J. U., the way he signed letters and notes) the New York Jewish novelist and social commentator Henry Bech.

Bech appeared on the scene concurrently with *Of The Farm*, after stories from his perspective, beginning with "The Bulgarian Poetess," appeared in the *New Yorker*. His incarnation permitted Updike to deliver some well-aimed blows to the literati, as in the hilarious "Appendix B," where most of the "in" quarterlies and literary logrollers are exposed. Bech's character and appurtenances and publications are fashioned as carefully as Achilles's shield, in order to deflect, it seems, the pressures of a crisis building in Updike—there are confessions of this in his essays—just before he wrote *Of The Farm*.

Bech is a native New Yorker, a blocked Jewish writer with a physical resemblance to Mailer, a backhand there, and in Bech Updike fashioned a self-deprecating comic double able to turn aside critical animus. The animus began, I believe, because Updike's *Olinger* prose, as it struck senses nurtured in the staid gray shades of the fifties, conveyed the flashy canter of a trick rider who knows he has the goods and is flaunting it, a show-off. That was one side of it; but worse, for the cognoscenti, was Updike's open adherence to Christianity and his reference to it in his fiction.

A Christian guy with the goods who is flaunting it doesn't represent Updike's intent or state of mind, if one can trust the glimpses he's given of himself, during the era of this early work, in later essays. Here, from *Hugging the Shore*, about his entry to an anthology pompously titled, *This Is My Best*: "The story lengthily titled 'Packed Dirt, Churchgoing, A Dying Cat, A Traded Car,' was written, as I remember, in the spring of 1961, at a time when my wits seemed sunk in a bog of anxiety and my customary doubts that I could write another word appeared unusually well justified."[4] Here in Updike's admission lies the fear that is Bech's actual state.

This dates from approximately a year before Updike wrote *Of The Farm*, as one discovers in *Picked-Up Pieces*. The confession is all the more striking when it is placed in a period of such prodigious output the pour of pages seemed unstoppable: *The Carpentered Hen* to *Of The Farm*—four novels, two short-story collections, two books of verse, three children's books, and a book of nonfiction in a decade.

To a writer as prolific as Updike, however, a week without words can seem a Sahara. Some writers go through droughts of months; others, like Bech, sit silent for years. Perhaps the most acute overview of Updike during those years is recorded by the person in the closest working relationship with him, his editor at the *New Yorker*, William Maxwell. In a *Paris Review* interview twenty years later, Maxwell says that watching Updike bear down on page proofs "was an education in how to refine language to the point where it almost becomes something else. The pure practised effectiveness and verve of an Olympic athlete is what it often reminded me of."[5]

As for *Of The Farm*, when I examine it now, at a remove from the heat a novel generates at its appearance, the passages that reviewers saw as overwritten seem necessary islands of reorganization and reflection—the limits to which Joey's mind is able to extend at the moment; after all, it's *his* book. As here, when his mowing of the meadow is interrupted by rain, and in the shelter of the house a rearrangement begins; he looks out a window, then notes: "Its panes were strewn with drops that as if by amoebic decision would abruptly merge and break and jerkily run downward, and the window screen, like a sampler half-stitched, or a crossword puzzle invisibly solved, was inlaid erratically with minute, translucent tesserae of rain."[6]

The only fifty-cent word, tesserae, is accurate from a pictorial artist's point of view (Joey, an advertising executive, has the painterly eye of early Updike narrators), and by means of the verbal impasto of this passage flaring away from the rest of the scene, if I may, the entire novel starts to turn. In the next sentence, in fact, Joey states: "A physical sense of ulterior mercy overswept me and led me to turn."[7]

Here, in a few plain simple words, the vague light of a transcendent moment is transformed into prose—and so effectively it might be the reason certain reviewers underwent a rage of envy: put out the light and then put out The Light. Tesserae are the tiles employed in the mosaics of early Christian iconography, and the word is a clue to the concluding artful statement that stands at the heart of Christian doctrine: that God's grace (unmerited favor or mercy) works in a sovereign, ulterior sense to cause repentance, a turning, here borne into consciousness by the artful patterns formed by a life-giving external source, rain. Could the acknowledgement of such doctrines cause critical animus?

A mature Updike, in a speech accepting an award for *Rabbit Is Rich*, said, "Surely this smiling audience harbors more than one young heart ardently wishing that the gray-haired apparition at this lectern will, like the doddering Emperor Achon of Azania in Evelyn Waugh's novel *Black Mischief*, instantly perish under the weight of his newly bestowed crown."[8] Though Updike delivered his mischievous remark in 1982, twenty years after *Of The Farm*, in the witty offhand that is a trademark, his acknowledgment of the killer instinct of envy (and his naming of it on this occasion) suggests a familiarity with it, including an artistic strategy that in its design disarms the instinct by stating it in the open, standing before an envying public audience.

At the center of *Of The Farm* rests a sermon delivered by a young Lutheran pastor at the rural church Joey and his mother attend on the Sunday of the weekend Joey is mowing her meadow. The sermon is presented in paraphrase, to keep us from being distracted by the speaker or his language, so we retain its relevant points, and it would be negligent to ignore them. The minister says that in reaching out to Eve "Adam commits an act of faith," and that his responsibility to Eve (a thought derived from Karl Barth, who is quoted) is "kindness."[9] Joey is separated from his Eve, or first wife, Joan (the name of the wife in the Maples stories, *Too Far to Go*), who seems the perfect partner for him, at least partly due to his mother's judgment, but he has left her for another wife, Peggy, a person his mother can barely endure.

Suddenly the reader is suspended by an application not carried to its conclusion, but hovering like a half-formed thought: Is Joey's leaving Joan for Peggy an act of faith? Of kindness? Adultery and divorce are the moral dilemmas Updike explores—or the betrayals caused by adultery and divorce are recapitulated everywhere in his work. Joey is now married to Peggy and is attempting to steer her gifted son (an encapsulated young Updike) toward equilibrium.

This could be viewed as kindness, but what about Joey's three natural children, who are discussed in only one scene, in terms bordering on the sentimental? In *Of The Farm*, we aren't as aware of the trail of broken children as in *Couples* or the Maples stories, but the loss Joey's children must feel sends a resonance through the book that, because it remains unresolved, is indeed depressing.

"We know how the lowly earthworm aerates the soil," the minister says in his sermon, now quoted directly for the point he is about to make: "Likewise, language aerates the barren density of brute matter with the penetrations of the mind, of the spirit."[10]

This sounds like Updike, and is indeed one of his credos, as he states in his poem "Earthworm."[11] At points in the novel, Joey heaps laudatory language on Peggy in the manner of "Archangel," a story from *Pigeon Feathers*; and when Joey is mowing his mother's meadow, in the passage already noted, the conclusion he reaches in the next sentence, overtly sexualized by the flecked tractor and hiplike seat, is: "My wife is a field."[12]

Meaning Peggy, right? The ambiguity seems intentional: either to be seeded or mowed, plowed or managed, like Joan, Joey's first wife. But the rest of the novel doesn't suggest that we will recall this passage (and others) in the midst of the minister's sermon. I can't help wondering, however, whether I'm viewing acts of faith and kindness or the opposite.

Further ambiguities hover over Joey's wives and his intentions toward them, adumbrating (another Updike word) the dark core of depression present in the text. And what seems finally conveyed by *Of The Farm* is a crisis in Updike about the body of work he's married to and responsible for. Will he remain the vulnerable writer with an Olympian's skill, hugging the sheltered shore of Olinger, or become distanced, à la Bech, and revert to jokes when cornered, or perhaps take on a further cast, as in Nabokov (a writer Updike admired, we learn from his essays), by a penchant to shock?

II

The choice Updike made at this juncture and the route his career took is apparent in his next novel, *Couples*.[13] It feels looser and less well written than the earlier books, with longeurs of description that tend to have a feel of indulgence, and what attracted its large readership, surely, are its explicit descriptions of sexual acts of various sorts among a variety of partners. A round of wife-and-husband swapping is embarked on, with a focus on graphic detail, in spite of Updike's later disclaimers about accuracy and honesty. I believe I understand, in an intellectual sense, what Updike is up to; in interviews from this period and in later ones, besides essays scattered through his career, he has confessed he is a Christian—a brave stance for a late twentieth-century writer to take—and *Couples* is at least partly his take on Christianity in suburban America in the late sixties. It's *awful*.

His autobiography, *Self-Consciousness*, confirms that confession, and I'll refer to it in its proper place. As Updike says in interviews, he has rested in the shelter of Christianity most of his life, and the alert reader recognizes the inclusion of Christian iconography and symbols and apologetics, even doctrine, in nearly every book, not just *Of The Farm* and *Couples*. But in *Couples*, for the first time Christianity ruffles the surface in unpleasant ways.

In Updike's running disquisition on the "yes, but" attitude that critics took toward his work ("Yes, it's good, but . . . ."), he stated in a 1968 *Paris Review* interview about *Couples*, taking first the negative branch, "No, in *Couples*, to a religious community founded on physical and psychical interpenetration, but—what else shall we do, as God destroys our churches."[14]

God destroys them, not people? Updike defines this God as the God of "ultimate power . . . the God of earthquakes and typhoons, of children starving. A God who is not God the Creator is not very real to me, so that, yes, it certainly is God who throws the lightning bolt [the Congregational Church in Tarbox burns down when struck by lightning] and this God is above the nice god, above the god we can worship and empathize with."[15]

Is this nice god or "the god we can worship and empathize with" Updike's creation? Or society's, since he employs the royal we (a possible candidate for the editorial "we," according to Twain, is a man with a tapeworm) or is it the god of the contemporary church? Updike implies that the God of "ultimate power" is a source of catastrophic supremacy, and since I see a door that he's left open, it seems permissible to step through it and examine his statement in terms of historic Christianity, as elements of its centenary shifts appear in his work.

The nice god Updike mentions is the god of modern theology, rendered approachable by his denaturing through higher criticism, via Schleiermacher, Delitzsch, Tillich, and others. He is subject to humanity's adjudication of him. This god, rather than the one defined in the Hebrew and Greek Scriptures, is built on the philosopher-theologians' subjective definitions of him. He is a god who is, as a friend used to say, "Whatever you make him."

He is the god that canny, case-hardened alcoholics refer to as the Higher Power, sometimes with a wink, meaning *I'm* the Higher Power. Though higher critics come robed in academic respectability, their outlook is essentially the same as the alcoholic's: I've got my own better view of God. And their suppositions about texts, which are impossible to prove, tend to supplant the texts themselves. The "twelve steps" become a religion.

If this seems a far reach about a trend that perhaps had altruistic beginnings—sound textual research—its negative results are everywhere evident. American churches split over trends it introduced, and the intellect and essayist, Peter Viereck, who produced a dozen books, brought into focus, step by prescient step, in *Metapolitics: The Roots of the Nazi Mind*, the effect of higher criticism in Germany reducing Christianity to a nullity that paved the way for the Third Reich and its religion. Viereck was also a poet, so he was aware of the persuasive power of words and texts and, like any poet of the era in which he wrote, the forties into the seventies, he knew the *sine qua non* was academic respectability. Forget biblical theology, based on the Scriptures, and instead read or study at the right seminary under the right professors and make sure you quote them.

In *Couples*, Updike is ostensibly probing the absence of the "real" God. But the premises of his examination are Barthian, so he places God so far above "the god we worship" he is catastrophically distanced, unreachable: the Thou of Buber, about whom one forms dim suppositions based on Buber, whose followers are drawn to Emerson, Thoreau, and D. H. Lawrence, all of whom are led by "nature." What Updike and his fictional analogues sidestep is a historical outlook; those who have worshiped a "jealous" God because he is fearful—a consuming fire. They worship him (in spite of this) because he is also the only source of absolute mercy, as defined in dozens of ways in the words of Scripture, beginning with the Hebrew Bible. But in that text no Intermediary appears to absorb his inability to bear imperfection.

In *Couples*, Updike invites his readers to reexamine the fallacious views of utopian communes—the blasé superiority of his Tarbox couples akin to Oneida adherents—and communion in an adulterated church that has slept with every mythic entity. Here couples commune with one another in a sexual partnering Updike says they see as a new *communion*. In addition it seems he is charting further aspects of the fall in New England since Hawthorne—as he openly does in *Roger's Version*—while at the same time criticizing the idea of attempting to establish a nation on the lines of a commune, as in Soviet Russia, where he spent time early in his career.

Angela, angel and wife of Piet, the central character of *Couples*, is the daughter of a Unitarian minister (as Ruth in *Marry Me*, as the bride in *Pigeon Feathers*), and this minister's ineffectiveness suggests the degree to which the social gospel, taken up by Unitarian Transcendentalism, has unmanned the church. The vacuum of its contentless emptiness invites lightning bolts, and in *Couples*, as is usual in everyday life, no human being is harmed by lightning that is a common phenomenon of weather in the everyday world.

Updike also seems to be saying, whether intentionally or not, that grace abounds to the chiefest sinner. As one follows Piet (pronounced "Pete," Dutch for "Peter," the rock) bounding from bed to bed, one is aware of Updike's affection for Piet, as if his creator's blessings rest on him.

In the late sixties, before I was thirty, I may have been dumbly drawn, along with thousands of others, by the allure of what came to be known as the *Playboy* philosophy, but I was not then, nor will be, I pray, a proponent. I believe that most readers, especially those who happened on *Couples* in 1968, believed that philosophy was the governing agent of the novel—seek sexual pleasure with no limits, because that is what the Hefnerites in Chicago do.

The theology in Updike's work, present even in his poems, is primarily the theology of Kierkegaard and Barth. Both Kierkegaard and Barth are in the tradition of Kant and therefore are, in the nomenclature of philosophy, irrationalists. The noumenal and the phenomenal in Kant are entities that cannot be united, except that the amorphous and unknowable noumenal can be contained, for Kant anyhow, by the global apprehension of his own mind, like jelly in a jelly glass.

Kierkegaard, responding to Hegel's "mere conceptual" existence, proposed an irrational leap of faith, which runs counter to most Christian doctrines, and debates continue about Kierkegaard's "Christianity." He was the first to articulate existentialism, although many before him lived it, and W. H. Auden, a devotee who called attention to Kierkegaard in America, said that one can read the whole of Kierkegaard and come away believing that human beings do not have a body, meaning his writings are cerebral and over-spiritualized and ignore the central grand mystery of the Christian message: God in a body like yours.

Barth (Karl, not John), the Swiss-German theologian who is known as the originator of neoorthodoxy, implies in portions of his writings that unless the Spirit illuminates a passage of Scripture for the individual, then that passage (to be reductive) isn't relevant—a concept that invites endless equivocation in anybody able to think, and an individual's speculations about Scripture—and his or her personal illumination, perhaps—may supplant Scripture itself.

Through the character of Piet, as with the Lutheran pastor in *Of The Farm*, Updike brings his knowledge of theology to bear on the scruples of the characters in *Couples*. In *Couples*, however, he employs for the first time not his native Lutheran background but his own brand of Dutch Reformed Calvinism, which is a continental twin to the New England Puritanism that rests like a deconstructed predecessor under the collapsing couples coupling in *Couples*.

Piet attends the Tarbox Congregational Church that burns down after it is hit by the lightning bolt (as one burned down in Ipswich, where Updike was then living), and both his person and the church have similar but varying religious antecedents. New England Congregational churches were once Calvinistic. The Pilgrims, British outcasts who first emigrated from England to Holland, were hyper-Puritans who focused on piety and tended to mistrust, after their experience with Anglican rule, any church government that wasn't local and congregational: they were, you might say, in Plato's negative definition, democratic in church polity.

The term "Puritan" derives from those who wished to purify the English worship service of its remaining vestiges and vestments of the once-universal Roman Catholic Church. The Puritans of Massachusetts Bay Colony were mostly Presbyterian in government, with ascending levels of Presbyteries, and then Assemblies or Synods. In continental Europe, in Geneva, the Calvinism of the Swiss-French theologian Calvin affected church and municipal government, not because Calvin established a theocracy, as poorly read scholars surmise; what happened was if his church council learned that one of its members was guilty of a crime that fell under the authority of the civil government, they turned the offender over to the civil authorities.

"What does it matter if a tradition no one identifies with any longer is unjustly disparaged," Marilynne Robinson writes in her superb essay "Puritans and Prigs" from the collection, *The Death of Adam.* "If history does not precisely authorize the use we make of the word 'Puritanism,' we all know what we mean by it, so what harm is done? Well, for one thing we make ourselves ignorant and contemptuous of the first two or three hundred years of one major strain of our own civilization."[16]

Calvinists were common in Holland, where the Pilgrims found free sanctuary, and a few Hollanders made a separate migration, settling Nieuw Amsterdam, later New York under British rule. The Dutch Reformed Calvinism in America has its twentieth-century locus in Grand Rapids, Michigan, a location many of its members refer to with amused affection as New Jerusalem. Piet is from Michigan, from this Dutch Reformed milieu, and when, after the book appeared, Updike was called Calvinist by his critics, he protested, "No, I'm Lutheran!"

To which one might respond, from the corridor of historic Christianity, "Yes, but—" Luther was at least as Calvinistic as Calvin. Faith is a gift of God alone, Luther wrote, not based on personal merit or come-forward-and-make-a-decision, and faith as a gift is the heart of Calvinism, once the misunderstandings and uninformed polemics against the name are set aside. Luther was the first to take up pen as cudgel against Christian humanism, which mellowed Scripture through the early classics (not later ones, while Calvin tended to revere the classics), and offered humankind autonomy in the matter of salvation. This was the eventual outworking of the Dutch theologian, Erasmus. In *The Bondage of the Will*, Luther refutes Erasmus and denies free will in regeneration, or making a "decision for Christ." Luther's view is known as justification by faith, and faith is a gift of God, bestowed by the Holy Spirit, as in St. Paul's epistle to the Ephesians.

Updike may be slyly suggesting in *Couples* that it takes a Midwestern Calvinist, an outsider, to set in perspective the slippage of New England Calvinism, as Piet does, picking up on its freewill autonomy. Its course along the East Coast was degenerative, declining from a mere work ethic to nature worship. The Calvinism that arrived with the Puritans and Pilgrims (separatist Congregationalists) went from Unitarianism to Transcendentalism to pantheism to Sophia theology—where ecology becomes The Religion (the earth Mother or Brother or God, Gaia or Sophia), and subordinates human beings to its imperatives, as in the unscientific cant of the heated-up earth advocates who, at the top, are bent on establishing "alternative" corporations in order to profit from the religious scare they induce.

The tracing of the deterioration of Pilgrim faith would be a valid course for *Couples* to take, but I suspect Updike doesn't resonate with Calvin as he does with Barth. Calvinistic doctrines of predestination and election and perseverance of the saints—mistakenly codified in some evangelical circles as "eternal assurance" and by the Catholic Church as the prerogative of confessors under its wing; once a Catholic, always a Catholic, to heaven's gates.

About election or the calling of the elect, as Calvin derived it from passages in Scripture—his most abhorred and debated doctrine—he himself said it's best not to look too deeply into the matter or bring it to bear on others, because its resolution is in the mind of God alone. That there are death-bent unreachables, however, is borne out in nearly every decade of history, as in the present, using passenger jets and strapped-on bombs to destroy innocent others. Calvin believed that what was important in his theology, as it should be in any, was not God's omnipotence but the riches sent to earth in Christ, and wrote, "This is what we should in short seek in the whole of scripture: truly to know Jesus Christ, and the infinite riches that are comprised in him and are offered to us by him from God the Father."[17]

As Marilynne Robinson notes in her essay, "While Calvinists spoke of an elect, Leninists and suchlike have spoken of an elite. The two words come from the same root and mean the same thing. Their elect were unknowable, chosen by God in a manner assumed to be consistent with his tendency to scorn the hierarchies and overturn the judgments of this world. Our elites are simply, one way or another, advantaged."[18]

The doctrines propounded by Calvin, along with forgiveness in Christ, do not permit unbridled sin so grace will abound. God forbid, as the Apostle Paul says on that point. Certainly Christians have abused these doctrines, as many have abused the doctrine of grace, as others abuse corporate accounts or trusting investors or tenets of the Qur'an, and a terrifying dramatization of how twisted Calvinistic misinterpretations can become is found in *The Private Memoirs and Confessions of a Justified Sinner*, by James Hogg (a.k.a. The Ettrick Shepherd), published in 1824.

These misinterpretations, however, apparently didn't interest Updike. Piet's sexual resilience and his name, pronounced plain "Pete" but in spelling approximating piety (which in its original sense means "works in action"), suggest a mantle of grace. Piet seldom feels more than dim guilt about his sexual diversity. I don't think any reader would say he repents of adultery, as even Reverend Dimmesdale, the cause of the Scarlet Letter, does.

What *Couples* conveys is the paradox of neoorthodoxy, and perhaps this was Updike's burden of illumination: its "kind" character can lead to destruction. All Christian doctrine comes down to this: *love your neighbor*, period. Going to bed with her may stem from a love-limned motive but it's not so great for her husband, one suspects—or for the children of both families, as the disruptions in *Couples* convey. This "law of love," as some grace-driven, American evangelicals call it, can undergird any infamous or heinous action to gratify its own desires—in fact, any definition an individual gives it: "I am my own law, I am the higher power"—and a practical outworking of the attitude is apparent in high school and other shootings.

And if my neighbor wants revenge, or simply doesn't like me or the way I look, he will work that out on terms that to him seem *his* right. Which means he might appear in a fast-food restaurant firing an automatic: "Here's what you get, world!" That's the reaction the antinomian impulse inspires: each his own lawmaker and upholder of a single, personal law. I bring Apocalypse!

It's the impulse that has emptied America of moral conduct. Historical Christianity, like Judaism, was a religion of ethics and morals. It is only in this century that the idea has become current that grace displaces sin no matter how promiscuous. One is indeed redeemed by grace, yes, and grace is sufficient to cover any sin; but grace is also sufficient to restrain it, and when it leaps past that, grace is sufficient to allow a person to recognize his or her state in comparison to the infinite perfection of God in Christ. There has to be a walk or a way of life, a continuing confession of frailty to temptation, if one is engaged in a life of redeemed change.

If in the past a Christian life took a headlong plunge into lawlessness—the opposite of law, as reprobation is the opposite of grace—and remained there, the Christian began to question the validity of his or her redemption: Am I hopelessly reprobate? This questioning, when turned with unremitting force on one's self, was called "morbid introspection." Christians did not pass off sin, or laugh it off, or drink to dull the guilt it brought. It was a grievous matter the church attended to if the individual didn't. The law was important not because you earned merit by obeying it but because it was a hedge, the only wise one, against destruction. It was also a measure of progress, when tested against the perfect obedience of Christ.

There are present-day Christians who scoff at this and their attitude has helped empty the culture of ethical content—the preserving salt necessary to keep any culture from rotting. The "let go and let God" free grace attitude has undone what newscasters call fundamentalists but are actually antinomian dispensationalists, such as Jim Bakker, from a Dutch Reformed background, and Jimmy Swaggart, a charismatic who told his followers Calvinism was Satanic. It is the attitude that focuses on "I" and "me," and follows the same self-centered gratification that governed the sixties of *Couples*—if-it-feels-good-do-it, an attitude discredited by most of its adherents in the present as they advance in the corporate world—and is the engine that governs that scary film, *The Apostle*.

I'm not sure Updike hoped to dramatize the schizophrenia of antinomianism, but he did. What hasn't helped is how some of his novels have given intellectual credibility to antinomianism as no Calvinist could. The most a reader who enters *Couples* from the Reformed tradition it presumably follows can say is, "Yes, this exposes my potential sin, but—" Again, *Yes, but*.

In a recent essay, "Lost in Fiction," by Alexander McCall Smith, the Scots novelist and mystery writer who is the author also of sixty books, Smith laments the way critics and readers chide him for certain actions of his characters, as if they're real people he has used the wrong way, and says: "The conclusion that I am increasingly drawn to is that the world of fiction and the world of flesh-and-blood people are not quite as separate as one might imagine. Writing is a moral act: What you write has a real effect on others, often to a rather surprising extent."[19]

It would be well to note that Updike, struggling under the stresses of neoorthodoxy, has more than once warned the American church ("Pigeon Feathers," *A Month of Sundays*, *Roger's Version*) about the clerics we might expect if its doctrines are carried to their logical conclusions. And we shouldn't forget John Gardner's warning of 1980, already mentioned, that the message he found in Updike, "again and again, is a twisted version of the message of his church, neo-Orthodox Presbyterianism. Christ has saved us; nothing is wrong; so come to bed with me."[20]

Updike might respond, "Yes, but I'm not a Presbyterian; I'm a Lutheran who became a Congregationalist, and now I'm an Espicopalian." Yes, but his novels and stories and essays and autobiography over and over acknowledge his indebtedness to

Barthian theology, and Barth, as Gardner knew, was a neoorthodox Lutheran-Presbyterian.

The effect of the couplings in *Couples*, from tragic to comic (the last pair to join the game dive into a mound of dirty clothes), finally leaves the reader with too much laundry to sort. Few critics sensed that Updike found the coupling unsound. Because of the graphic elaboration in some of the scenes, an elderly book dealer in New York, who handled the work of the expatriates, including Joyce and Henry Miller, called *Couples* "a dirty book."

Why? It conveys the attitude of an earlier generation, as the work of Mailer, the detractor of Updike, does. Both find prurient pleasure, it seems, in presenting men and women, but especially women, sweatily busy at the naughtiness of sex—the voyeuristic strain of a generation basically Victorian, as exemplified by their headmaster, Edmund Wilson. His single fictional work, *Memoirs of Hecate County*, was much admired by Updike. While Mailer and Updike were writing their widely received novels, *Deer Park* to *An American Dream* and *Rabbit, Run* to *Couples*, an openness and sense of equity, enshrined in blues and folk music, was gaining currency in a new generation. A former student of my alma mater, of the era of Updike, had moved to Chicago and become the purveyor of a new publication, *Playboy*—the benchmark of American male, hairy-handed voyeurism.

From 1961 to 1964, partially aided by drugs, college students became iconoclasts of Eisenhowerish prudery (also known as Mamieism), because it had the identical feel of the hypocrisy they experienced in church. Updike and Mailer, busy at their books, missed this, I think. If students of the early sixties weren't quite letting it all hang out, they were about to, and an unwritten code was not to reveal a relationship in salacious embroidery, much less invite somebody to join in, even conversationally. IT was IT, its intimacy limited to its participants, often in an attitude of condign and frank friendliness, if not affection.

Couples illustrated the power of the pen over the sword; a year after it appeared, and was reissued in paperback in a choice of colors, magenta or cobalt, or baby blue and pink, as if reaching to both sides in a display of the two, theologian and hedonist, of its author, the sixties began to give and crack. I was traveling at the time and found people in the Midwest acting like couples from Tarbox.

Ideas can't be enacted by a populace until the ideas are embodied and dramatized—that is the power of the stage and fiction, not to mention the totalitarian grip of TV. With *Couples*, the philosophy of *Playboy* moved into the hearts of heartland America. The people there became swingers along Hefner's lines, Piets and Foxys, numbed.

III

In 1969, I stepped into the bathroom of a house in the heart of the Midwest and saw a paperback copy of *Couples* splayed open, face down on the floor—one of the pink versions. Then as I was entertained at a barbecue Freddy Thorne could have overseen, I wondered if Updike was aware of his effect. As it turned out, the owner of the house was sleeping with his neighbor's wife, as the evening's events revealed, and somebody was maybe sleeping with his. A year later he and his wife were divorced, their neighbors were divorced, there were remarriages, and four families were displaced, the children divided up. It would be unseemly to say the cause of this was *Couples*, but I believe you could say *Couples* hit the gas on a trend, rather than the clutch or the brake.

There's a tendency in all, from Augustine to Harry Angstrom, to imitate rabbits. Even Harry, however, who doesn't wear Piet's mantle of grace, is restrained by circumstance, and eventually acknowledges, by way of his angst, some need for self-government. This happens in both *Rabbit Is Rich* and *Rabbit at Rest*, but the intellectuals and professionals of Tarbox (soon to be yuppies) and a similar crowd in Roger's version of Boston and a few clerics of *In the Beauty of the Lilies* don't seem to recognize the need. Is Updike implying that an intellectual Unitarian upbringing permits indulgences the proles can't pursue? Surely not, though the condescending superiority of the narrator of *Roger's Version* (a modern *Scarlet Letter*, as Updike says) suggests exactly that.

The angst-ridden adolescents of *Pigeon Feathers*—one of Updike's better books—such as the young man who does not want to hear about an afterlife that is kind of like the idea of Abraham Lincoln's goodness living after him, but rather of a resurrection of the kind expressed in Updike's poem, "Seven Stanzas at Easter,"[21] seems, in *Couples*, to have surrendered.

In *Marry Me*, he partly returns, and if his communions are comparable to Piet's, they have a not so commendable purpose: "With the sword of his flesh he had put the mockers to rout. Christ was revenged."[22] The man writing *A Month of Sundays*, the next novel after *Couples*, enters fully into a mocking Nabokovian tone, and must be Updike's most repellent character. With the appearance of *Witches of Eastwick* he appears to have joined the other team, and in *Roger's Version* he's absent. He has become the liberal Lutheran pastor abhorred by the adolescent of "Pigeon Feathers."

This break, this choosing of allegiances, the blue and pink division in Updike, occurs in *Couples*. Many of Updike's short stories, especially those that seem analogous to Updike's own marriage (the late Maples stories) and much of *In the Beauty of the Lilies*, regain again the visceral engagement and potential reach, even grandeur of *The Centaur*, *Pigeon Feathers*, *Of The Farm*, and portions of the *Rabbit* quartet (*The Coup*, *S*, *Brazil*, *Gertrude and Claudius*, *Seek My Face* and others are either other-cultural or less relevant to the issue); otherwise the spiritual struggle seems abandoned for a corresponding struggle with the flesh, a version of neo-Manichaeism.

Or Transcendentalism, mingled with Romantic hubris. In many passages in *Couples*, Updike, rubbing through as omniscient narrator, tries to establish a relationship with nature comparable to the one viewed by the narrator of "Leaves"—"sunlight falls flat at my feet like a penitent."[23] But in *Couples*, as in this passage seen through the eyes of the biochemist, Ken, Foxy's husband, the effort is obvious: you sense a mediator translating "cuckolded biochemist's consciousness" into cooked symbolism and experience a minor-key performance dependent on language:

> Expressways capillariously fed the humped dense center of brick red where the State House dome presided, a gold nucleolus. Dusty excavations ravaged the nearer ground. In the quad directly below, female students in bright spring dresses—dyed trace elements—slid along the paths between polygons of chlorophyll.[24]

In *Couples*, there is little sorrow and repentance, unless Bernadette Ong's return to her rosary is meant to convey that. Issues of Christian concern aren't undertaken with the life-and-death urgency of Updike's early work, but are dropped, turned into tentative introspection (see the jogging scene in *Rabbit Is Rich*), or translated into overt commentary, as in this exchange from *Marry Me*:

> "One nice thing about being a Unitarian, it doesn't saddle you with too much bourgeois morality." [So says Jerry, with irony, to his wife, Ruth]
> "Being a Lutheran doesn't seem to either." [Ruth]
> "It's not supposed to. We live by faith alone."[25]

The difference between this and the early work is the difference between Donne's early sermons and the escalating ladders of his poetry. That difference seemed, in the seventies, a regrettable loss, as a writer of extraordinary potential and power rested content on his ability to trace the contours of a culture's visible lapses.

I am as opposed (as Updike, I assume) to popular Christian writing of the pietistic, sanitized, untruthful bent; and to the act of dragging a pulpit into fiction—although Updike does this to admirable effect in *Pigeon Feathers*, *Of The Farm*, *Roger's Version*, *Marry Me*, and, to a certain extent, *Couples*. He has also imported the world of carpentry and biology, roughly digested, into *Couples*, and computer jargoning, slightly off-key, according to a software writer I know, into *Roger's Version*. In this last novel, the blandishments of liberal heretics are set against the nitwit belief (as communicated by Roger) of a young man committed to a too-realistic creational view of the world. Dim Dale. He's referred to in those words by Roger.

Which is to say that imports are made, at the author's discretion, and what is finally conveyed is a sense of Updike staring down from a magisterial height at the "unromantically round head" (implying Cromwellian Calvinism returning to Britain via New England) of the young American artist in "Still Life."[26] Or at the one-minded concerns of the boy in "Pigeon Feathers," and looking down with amused irony, not charity.

IV

Self-Consciousness arrives from the latter era of Updike's oeuvre as a gift.[27] In this autobiographical memoir he addresses many of the concerns already mentioned—which may be why the book was misunderstood, if not maligned, in politically inclined and therefore intolerant critical quarters. Actually, it's one of his better books, composed of chapter-long essays of reminiscence, each on a separate topic.

These seem the "three or four 'longish' ruminative essays in the 'Thoreauvian-Emersonian tradition'" Updike once mentioned he hoped someday to attempt. Two of these, "A Soft Spring Night in Shillington" and "Getting the Words Out," are perhaps the best examples we have of what it was like to come of age in America in the last half of the last century.

The first, "A Soft Spring Night in Shillington," takes place in April, the month of Updike's birth. Over the space of the essay, Updike spends an idle hour or so waiting for a piece of luggage he has lost on an airplane flight. It's to be delivered to him in his hometown, Shillington, Pennsylvania, by an airline employee. During the wait, while other members of his family attend a movie, Updike goes for a walk down familiar Shillington streets.

In one of those strokes of providence that seldom work in fiction, the movie his family is watching is *Being There*. Updike's essay is concerned with "being" and being where he is at the moment, in the here and now of the Shillington he left decades long ago. The star of the movie, Peter Sellers, the foremost comedian of Updike's generation, and one of the best mimics and impersonators, is no longer living. The author of the rather numb novel the movie is based on, Jerzy Kosinski is, in his savoring of cruelty, Updike's antithesis. A soft spring rain is falling, which is later interpreted: "Rain is grace; rain is the sky condescending to the earth; without rain there would be no life."[28] A reminder of the rain scene in *Of The Farm*.

On this night of grace, then, in Updike's life, he walks down a side street to his old neighborhood, to the house where he was born, the locus of his consciousness. He studies the house where his identity formed, and as he ruminates, the reader begins to see how concentric circles widen from the place that is the locus of *me* in each of us—the house that sheltered our development.

This is the best American essay on the prerogatives of place and its relationship to identity that I know. And since the identity examined is of a prominent writer, a definition of the prerogative of place in its relationship to writing is established, and I don't think a more eloquent examination of that relationship exists in twentieth-century American literature. The first location our consciousness adheres to, self-consciously or not, is the locus of being we rest within when we think, *Home*.

Dasein, Updike thinks, the "Why me?" of existence, or, "Why is it I exist here?" Standing under the marquee of the movie theater, after studying the house where he lived until he was thirteen, he recalls two sensations that remain from childhood: "The awareness of things going by, impinging on my consciousness, and then, all beyond my control, sliding away toward their own destination and destiny."[29] This does not inspire in him helplessness or fear; on the contrary: "To put myself to sleep, I would picture logs floating down a river and then over a waterfall, out of sight. Mailing letters, flushing a toilet, reading the last set of proofs—all have this sweetness of riddance."[30]

And:

> The second intimation of deep, cosmic joy . . . is really a variation of the first: the sensation of shelter, of being out of the rain, but just out. I would lean close to the chill windowpane to hear the raindrops ticking on the other side; I would huddle under bushes until the rain penetrated; I loved doorways in a shower. On our side porch, it was my humble job, when it rained, to turn the wicker furniture with its seats to the wall, and in these porous caves I would crouch, happy almost to tears, as the rain drummed on the porch rail and rattled the grape leaves of the arbor and touched my wicker shelter with a mist like the vain assault of an atomic army.[31]

A patch of description, one might say, but matchless, with the fictive freedom of defining a condition along lines nearly scientific, in a visionary sense of excited discovery:

> Early in his life the child I once was sensed the guilt in things, inseparable from the pain, the competition: the sparrow dead on the lawn, the flies swatted on the porch, the impervious leer of the bully on the school playground. The burden of activity, of participation, must plainly be shouldered, and has its pleasures. But they are cruel pleasures. There was nothing cruel about crouching in a shelter and letting phenomena slide by: it was ecstasy. The essential self is innocent, and when it tastes its own innocence knows that it lives forever. If we keep utterly still we can suffer no wear and tear, and will never die.[32]

Though tinged with Emersonianism, this is an Adamic credo. If Adam and Eve in their innocence had remained unmoved, incorruptible, they would have lived forever; we would never die. The world is fallen and hostile but the burden of participation (in every sense, including one's work in that world) must be shouldered. What is unstated is that Updike persevered as one of America's most prolific writers within that kernel of ecstatic identity under a shelter that lets through the world like a sieve.

A sense of shelter is, for him, at least in one sense, the ambusher's quiet. From it he gains the ability to observe and produce the "interlaced" world of imitative creation, the act of which is the Gloria of servitude.

To the "Why me?" that Updike poses, the reader comes to understand that because of the "humble job" he was assigned, and by performing that job in a regular, obedient manner he remained true to his "docile, good-child nature,"[33] and began to construct an otherworld on the porch of this house at the heart of his concentric circles.

A subsidiary benefit of the essay, for those who have followed Updike's work since the sixties, is that several early stories receive specific reference or location points. And the lyrically evocative *O, linger!* that Updike chose when he renamed Shillington is, we learn, a local family name.

The Shillington of Updike's youth is also an analogue to the locale of the Rabbit quartet, as we also learn, particularly *Rabbit, Run*. So in the perambulations of the essay the important precincts of those locales are traced by the person who has built dozens of books up from them. The essay, traveling with the Jamesian rhythmic precision of Updike's best prose, is wonderful in its generosity, and in addition often moving.

The generosity of spirit Updike has extended to other writers, in his hundreds of reviews over the years, has its origins here. The central section of Shillington in which he grew up is the given of his identity, and he lived not only with his parents—one a volatile writer, one a self-effacing high school teacher—both of whom changed, but also his grandparents, who changed and died; even the status of the family changed when the extended ménage moved to the Hoyer homeplace in nearby Plowville—"a name that is an embarrassment to me still," Updike has written.

But this central section of Shillington did not change through Updike's high school years (as it has changed little since) or for the maturing Updike, who began to view himself partly as the hero at its center—"At the age of seventeen I was poorly dressed and funny-looking, and went around thinking about myself in the third person"—but neither hostile nor an antihero.[34] He was an only child with a foundational home that remained stable, and he was the focal point of two generations who mostly wanted to extend blessings, as in "The Blessed Man of Boston," and unqualified love to him.

"Getting the Words Out" is a study of the means by which Updike has been able to deliver a book or more a year over his tenure as a writer. Behind his productivity, we learn, is a stammer of the sort that hampered writers like Hemingway and Maugham. Updike comically suggests that the source of his problem is a neighborhood bully who called him an ostrich; Updike's speech began to fall apart when he tried to explain he wasn't. There is no doubt, after reading Updike's account of his stammer, that the stammer is partly the source of his search in each sentence for precision. "In most people there is a settled place they speak from; in me it remains unsettled, unfinished, provisional."[35]

And: "I continued . . . to get the words out—to get them out in the specialized sense of words to be printed, as smooth in their arrangement and flow as repeated revision could make them, words lifted free of the fearful imperfection and impermanence of the words we all, haltingly, stumblingly, speak."[36] And finally:

> My own style seemed to me a groping and elemental attempt to approximate the complexity of envisioned phenomena and it surprised me to have it called luxuriant and self-indulgent; self-indulgent, surely, is exactly what it wasn't—other-indulgent, rather. My models were the styles of Proust and Henry Green as I read them (one in translation): styles of tender exploration that tried to wrap themselves around the things, the tints and voices and perfumes, of the apprehended real. In this entwining and

gently relentless effort there is no hiding that the effort is being made in language.[37]

Another of the essays, "On Not Being a Dove," is an *apologia pro vita sua* for the stand that Updike, and Rabbit, too, in *Rabbit Redux*, took during the Vietnam conflict. This wasn't an actual war but a decimation of US troops limited by Marquis of Queensberry rules, and it divided the nation. Most writers were, of course, Doves, or claimed to be, since that appeared to be the official stand as proscribed by PEN—the political organization of Poets, Essayists, and Novelists. But Updike, in the stubborn way in which he has worked to honor the individuality he views as "self," didn't follow the official line. He did not join the collective lingo of the liberal camp, though he was perhaps more an actual liberal than most, shorn of the ambiguous anger and shilly-shallying of Robert Lowell, for instance, who accepted an invitation to the White House during Vietnam and then declined by writing a letter to the *New York Times*, not his host, and from that point adopted the Boston-New York stance based on the views of television pundits, where true news is sacrificed for slant and polemics—the examples of Dan Rather and the young reporter and his editor at the *New York Times* only the tip of the behind-the-scenes manipulation.

Updike was not a hawk either, as the title of his essay indicates, but had the gritty temerity to express the complex feelings most Americans experienced over the time of our engagement in Vietnam but didn't make the evening news as the protestors, the talking heads, and the doneés of celebrity did, as Hollywood pontificators now often do. Nor did he rephrase the platitudes of PEN, where he served on the board of directors. "Don't read your reviews/ A*M*E*R*I*C*A," he concluded a poem written in England in 1969: "You are the only land."[38]

The complex surety of this declaration lies inside the concentric circles radiating from the house in Shillington, and it is the likely reason, along with Updike's overt Christianity, that he never received the Nobel. There has been no writer in North America in the last fifty years more worthy, none who has built an oeuvre of his notability not only of fiction and poetry and children's books but critical reviews and essays of a distinction not seen in America since Edmund Wilson.

The Nobel, too, has clearly become politicized, as a glance at the nonawardees of the last few decades proves—not to Willa Cather, not to Nabokov, not to Auden, not to Graham Greene, and on and on—and is yet another example of the exclusionary intolerance exercised by those who fashion themselves as open-minded to diversity of every kind.

A section of *Self-Consciousness* devoted to Updike's father and his family, "A Letter to My Grandsons," is curiously bare, like a scaffold set around the skeleton of a building. The reminiscence largely lists records and facts and leaves the impression that Updike is evading the central subject of this book, his father, who plays an essential moving role in his early work.

Under the movie marquee in "A Soft Spring Night in Shillington," Updike says, "silhouettes in slickers and parkas once in a while walked by, and one of them even recognized me and stopped to talk, mostly about my father, who was still more vivid in the town than I could ever be."[39]

The residual competitiveness of that final phrase is difficult for a faithful reader of Updike to keep from circling. A tentative impression left by the statement suggested that Updike's best novel remained unwritten. It was to be a book that dealt with the influence of his father head-on, and would perhaps reveal aspects of fatherhood that had not been touched on in American fiction, since Updike's genuine love for his father is transparent. There is an intimation of this potential at the end of *Rabbit Is Rich*, when the wife of Rabbit's son, Nelson, places Rabbit's first granddaughter in Rabbit's lap, and also in the soaring ending of *Rabbit at Rest*—with Nelson present in the flesh, to Rabbit's end in death.

If Updike didn't write that novel, he did in his fiction make it permissible for American men to love their fathers. The fifties taught us to humor or resent them; the sixties to question their authority; the seventies to discard them. If Updike offered no further contribution to American letters, or gave his readers no other gift, the permission to love one's father is enough.

V

Updike has, of course, conferred much more. The extent of his contribution can be measured by the Rabbit quartet. The four novels, set in a fictional approximation of Shillington, a semisuburb of Reading, unite the halves of Updike's career that parted between *Of The Farm* and *Couples*.

For thirty years, Updike followed the sidestepping and back-sliding and achievements of Harry Angstrom, also known as "Rabbit," for the "breadth of white face, the pallor of his blue irises, and a nervous flutter under his brief nose."[40] Rabbit was a high school basketball star who married early, and in *Rabbit, Run* Updike conveyed the constrictions and angst suffered by Harry and his wife Janice during the Eisenhower years. The thoughtless and terrible drowning of their first child narrows the focus of Rabbit's restless energy—a horror-tale version of Eliot's death by drowning.

Rabbit Redux occurs a decade later, at the end of the sixties. Harry, now a linotype operator, undergoes the humiliation of Janice taking up with a car salesman. And then, partly through his own inertia, Harry becomes involved with a young woman and a frenzied black man who usher him into the black-and-white wonderland of the sixties. Harry, now a conservative workingman, takes the side of America in its involvement in Vietnam. The novel is set against the moon shot of that era, while separate satellites surrounding Rabbit, including his son Nelson and his mother, go off on their own orbits, some into oblivion. But Harry and Janice eventually touch down, linked again, at the end of the novel—the last word of which reflects the tentative experiments and speech of the late sixties: "O.K.?"

Most critics missed the complexity of its interleaving, I believe, and misjudged it, several still complaining it is the slackest of the quartet, but it seems to me Updike is at the height of his powers here and presents his most ambitious, compassionate story, with the possible exception of *The Centaur*. In *Rabbit Is Rich*, a belated prizewinner (the prizes should have gone to *Run* or *Redux*), Rabbit is a successful entrepreneur—a salesman of Toyotas during the energy crunch of Jimmy Carter. This period of double-digit interest in America enables Rabbit, now running his wife's father's automobile agency, to invest in gold and become rich. His son, Nelson, meanwhile, has to get married, as Rabbit once did, and gets hooked on coke. Though the novel fizzles in the direction of *Couples* near its end, it is the most amusing of the Rabbit quartet.

Rabbit at Rest is the most seamlessly whole, with its own amusements. Harry, now lumpily overweight and hooked on candy, leads a semiretired life of golf and condos and investments, and ultimately dies from a seriocomic gesture too wonderful to disclose. What is remarkable about this final Rabbit novel are its elegiac descriptions, of nature and the American landscape—equal to any in American fiction, including the best of Fenimore Cooper's elegiac prose poems—when Cooper is not purposely striking an elegiac pose.

The passages in Updike achieve their power from our sense of inhabiting a consciousness as it records its last views of the world before it closes down—a remarkable feat, again, by Updike, and my next favorite of the quartet. I once prodded him for a *Rabbit Resurrected* (or even the *Rural Rabbit* he once promised) but other than the view we have of him, through Nelson's eyes, in the long short story, "Rabbit Revisited," there will be no more Harry Angstrom—a figure who marked off the last four decades of American history as no other character in literature has.

At the final textual parting of "A Soft Spring Night in Shillington," after the lost luggage is placed in the trunk of his mother's car, Updike's walk is onto Rabbit's turf: "Just the texture of the fine-pebbled Shillington alleys put me back into sneakers, slouching toward a basketball scuffle around a telephone pole."[41] Compare this with the opening of *Rabbit, Run*: "Boys are playing basketball around a telephone pole with a backboard bolted to it. Legs, shouts. The scrape and snap of Keds on loose alley pebbles seems to catapult their voices high into the moist March air blue above the wires."[42]

The remainder of the essay commemorates adolescent and high school pleasures of the kind Harry Angstrom, or Rabbit, unhappily married, laments giving up in *Rabbit, Run*. Updike's meditation in the midst of the falling rain ends with his acknowledging: "A fortunate life, of course—college, children, women, enough money, minor fame. But it had all, from the age of thirteen on, felt like not quite my idea. Shillington, its idle alleys and darkened foursquare houses, had been my idea."[43]

The compact source of memory contained in these few blocks of Shillington, in other words, formed the fixed idea or kernel of force that drove John Updike the person into the work that led to John Updike the author, who produced a multitude of books that will be turned to as long as readers exist.

Was it the docile, good-child nature in Updike that allowed him to get the words out? Certainly he responded to the joys and deprivations of his Shillington childhood with the discipline of treating writing as a humble job, including all the rigors and disappointments that a job of that nature involves. Writing did remain a humble job, as he related in a *Paris Review* interview: "Hemingway described literary New York as a bottle full of tapeworms trying to feed on each other. When I write, I aim in my mind not toward New York but toward a vague spot a little east of Kansas. I think of the books on library shelves, without their jackets, years old, and a countryish teenaged boy finding them, have them speak to him. The reviews, the stacks in Brentano's, are just hurdles to get over, to place the books on that shelf."[44]

His thoughts under the sheltering movie marquee turn to his father, a high school teacher analogous to George Caldwell, and there is a sudden confession: "I hid a certain determined defiance. I would not teach, I would not farm, I would not (deep down) conform. I would 'show' them, I would avenge all the slights and abasements visited upon my father—the miserly salary, the subtle tyranny of his overlords at the high school, the disrespect of his students, the laughter in the moviehouse at the name of Updike."[45]

Of this father, "his own father's failures and sorrow and early death had poured through him like rain through a broken window. And his, in turn, through me . . . ."[46] A remarkable confession when rain is the venue of grace this soft spring night. Emotion-driven directness of this kind is rare in memoirs and autobiography—an arena often entered by a writer who intends to apply cosmetic touches to an already polished image, usually by employing a variety of forms of self-protection, often generated by self-regard rather than self-consciousness.

The most disturbing self in *Self-Consciousness* is found in its final chapter, "On Being a Self Forever." Updike writes in the introduction to the book that he began the essays out of irritation, when he learned another writer was planning to do a biography of him. He says in the final essay "my writing here about my religion feels forced—done at the behest of others, of hypothetical 'autobiography' readers."[47]

In the mid-eighties, Updike, who elsewhere mentions his religious inclinations tend toward Unitarianism (though he was raised in the Lutheran church), became an Episcopalian. He is writing this essay, he says, "in an attempt to comfort some young reader as I was once comforted by Chesterton and Unamuno."[48] What is memorable, even extraordinary, about the essay is its unsparing record of aging, as that process has taken place in Updike. Some of this is troubling, as we hope to hold the brakes for him (imagining his last great book) but is never distancing, as the patches of Emersonian, materialist views of life after death are, once Updike skips past Paul's teaching of the resurrection.

"On Being a Self Forever" seems a rational attempt to explain the resurrection. It's slightly unsettling to watch a writer as wise as Updike, especially one who confesses he adheres to the Apostles' Creed ("I believe in . . . the resurrection of the body, and life everlasting"), try to formulate an explanation of his own, rather than recognizing the shocking enigma for what it is. The boy who confronted the Lutheran pastor is absent, along with the author of "Seven Stanzas at Easter," whose first stanza goes:

> Make no mistake: if He rose at all
> it was as His body;
> if the cells' dissolution did not reverse, the molecules
> reknit, the amino acids rekindle,
> the Church will fall.[49]

The doctrine of the resurrection is beyond explanation or imagination, and was not formulated by a human being; it is anticipated by the Prophets and carried out by Christ. Instead of revolving, then, as Updike does, around this eschatological conundrum that logic can neither validate nor dismiss, why not quote its primary teacher, Christ, or 1 Corinthians, chapter 15, mentioned only glancingly by Updike. If any sense resides in the hair-raising doctrine, it will come from that source. When Updike doesn't follow that venue in his concluding essay, one is led to suspect that his adherence to the neoorthodoxy of Barth is fixed.

Kierkegaard won't talk about God in generalities, he states, only in particulars, yet God remains so unknowable Kierkegaard can't name those particulars, except to set them in dramatizations through a variety of biblical and human characters and personas and pen names, and then hits the trampoline in a leap into faith. In spite of any disclaimers philosophers or textual critics invoke, their emphasis often falls on personal opinion or individual revelation—me rather than the body of commentary, exegesis, and teaching that has been built up over the centuries by writers and scholars in the church.

Updike has said his definition of a Christian is one who can confess the Apostles' Creed. Then recognition of what the "holy

Catholic Church" has produced on creeds since the third and fourth centuries, in its attempt to align the church with Scripture, seems in order. There exists, of course, a tradition in turning from the teachings of the church and church fathers, from the Reformers and counter-Reformers, to the traditions of a denomination, as suggested by the narrator in *A Prayer for Owen Meany*, who prefers The Book of Common Prayer to the Bible because it's "so much more orderly."[50]

I can appreciate the wryness of that and at the same time recognize that what the church fathers and translators and theologians over the centuries have attempted to do is order this seeming disorder into a set of teachings accepted by most Protestant denominations. The matter of church government, whether papal or Episcopal or Presbyterian (or the independence of Baptists and Congregationalists), once had little to do with that basic set of compact and, yes, emotionally loaded doctrines. Deviations from them have always existed, and have generally been refuted by church councils, often in the form of creeds or confessions. This was true at least until the nineteenth century, when the church seems to have decided that science and a form of pseudoscience, academic research (I mean particularly higher criticism), could formulate doctrinal explanations as valid as any the historic church reached through wrestling with scriptural texts.

When Updike uses the Apostles' Creed as a standard for Christianity, he leaves confessors wondering about his interpretation. Its first statement, "I believe in God, the Father Almighty, Maker of heaven and earth" is hardly reconcilable, for instance, with Updike's asides on earth theory, peppered through his essays and reviews over the years. The concept of an instantaneous appearance of the universe, as posited by astrophysicists, and recent theories of a young earth, as posited by younger astrophysicists (as pointed out by the astrophysicist John Polkinghorne), draws science closer to the church than Updike seems to care to do.

He repeats the mantra of billions of years in the tone of Carl Sagan, the TV prophet who kept insisting there was life on other planets, even when the gathered scientific data proved him, in every instance, dead wrong. In one sense, any theory of the origin of the universe is valid, since no human being was present to record it— though few would hold to the theory of the world resting on pillars or supported on the back of a god. This is myth, and the teachings derived from Scripture over the history of the Christian Church have not had concourse with myth, until this century. God is recorded as saying, "Let there be light!" and *bang*, there was light. Maybe it was a *big* bang.

Updike seems to want to share in the heritage of historic Christianity, always a literate and literary religion—from its inspired Mosaic foundations through Chaucer and Shakespeare and Bradstreet and Chesterton and Unamuno and O'Connor and Dillard. To say you confess the Apostles' Creed and then to refute its declarations can only help promote the brainless attitudinizing of those who say they believe in spirituality but not religion, or in God but not what the Bible says about him, thereby removing the source of him himself, another way of saying *I* will define God and religion.

Updike's words build from or accrete around other words, as he has mentioned in reviews and essays, and he has been comforted by the Word and works written from within the Christian tradition. So it's baffling to see what seems a lack of interest in the dozens of different shades of belief and unbelief available in explicit words in Scripture, long before any existentialist lifted an anguished lament.

The Law and the Prophets and the Gospels are rational, fixed in history, wholly integrated, and their complexity foresees every form of attitudinizing (or clear-headed belief) the human mind can imagine, plus a few that were new to me. When Roger of *Roger's Version* patronizes the young computer hacker who believes (too rationally) he will be able to see God, for instance, Roger neglects to inform the reader about the tortured irrationality of the heretics who are his interest, and their inability to take in one clear prose sentence of Scripture, not to say its songs and poetry.

In an ultimate sense, Updike reflects more accurately than any writer the contemporary religious climate in America. His characters do not show any deep interest in the teachings of the Hebrew Bible, and their actions portray the present-day deviation from historic Christianity. Like many modern churchgoers, Updike seems to suggest at times that it is the culture that dictates the direction of ethics and self-government, while the church exists only to permit each individual to define his or her own way, picking up doctrine from the flock, as Barth suggests.

The epigraph to *Of The Farm* reads:

> Consequently, when, in all honesty, I've recognized that man is a being in whom existence precedes essence, that he is a free being who, in various circumstances, can only want his freedom, I have at the same time recognized that I can want only the freedom of others.[51]

This is Sartre, and it's noteworthy to recognize that when Sartre wished to dramatize the implications of a lack of freedom, he turned to the Judeo-Christian doctrine of damnation, and placed three people in the "No Exit" of hell. In a 1968 introduction to the Czech translation of *Of The Farm*, Updike refers to the above epigraph as a "stern blessing."

The "quartet of scattered survivors," he writes, "grope with their voices toward cohesion. And seek to give each other the stern blessing of freedom mentioned in the epigraph from Sartre. Let us hope that all nations will in their varying languages seek to bestow this blessing upon one another." This rather stilted pontification, so unlike Updike, may have been brought about by the blasts he was receiving from anti-Christian critics and doves, and isn't the hope for this kind of blessing another variation on Updike's early Shillington credo, "I would not (deep down) conform"?—though I have no doubt that he wanted others to enjoy the freedoms he enjoyed over his life as an American citizen, as not all writers seem to.

The reminiscence entitled "On Not Being a Dove" also hopes to recapture the atmosphere of the era in which Updike felt most fully his creative self, the Ipswich idyll ("Ipswich belonged to Barth," he writes), and in one stroke he engineers the question a reader might ultimately ask:

> Our trips to the tonic north country squeezed us all into one smoky automobile and felt like a holiday back into adolescence. We would become a pack, welded together by the day's fatigue and bruises and beer. I seem to remember, on one endless drive back home in the dark down Route 93, while my wife sat in the front seat and her hair was rhythmically irradiated with light from opposing headlights. . . .[52]

All right, he does something to his backseat neighbor through her ski pants that arouses his "brotherly pride." This brings up the question raised by the elderly bookseller: Isn't this "dirty"? Or anyway low-down to women, especially his wife? When you consider the passage, the only one of its kind in the 250 pages of *Self-Consciousness*, it seems Updike is forcing the question by his almost gratuitous introduction of the incident—I *seem* to remember—and then the graphic detail I won't indulge in here.

The gratuitousness gives the passage a fulsome cast that causes one to wonder about its presence; if it weren't inserted to appease, in its "brotherly pride," some of the feminists whom Updike quotes in the same section, who have beleaguered him over his career.* Whatever the reasons, the passage delivers the jolt it seems Updike sometimes strives to achieve: shock.

I can't settle this final question for anyone, except by taking every passage in context, so I wouldn't presume to suggest I could

---

*In the Fawcett paperback Updike alters "brotherly pride" to "comradely pride."

settle it for my bookseller, much less another reader. And perhaps the best way to answer it is to allow Updike to have at it himself, in his own words; in "On Being a Self Forever," near the close of *Self-Consciousness*, he writes:

> I found a few authors, a very few—Chesterton, Eliot, Unamuno, Kierkegaard, Karl Barth—who helped me believe. Under the shelter (like the wicker chairs on the side porch) that I improvised from their pages I have lived my life. I rarely read them now; my life is mostly lived. God is the God of the living, though His priests and executors, to keep order and to force the world into a convenient mould, will always want to make Him the God of the dead, the God who chastises life and forbids and says No. What I felt, in that basement Sunday School of Grace Lutheran Church in Shillington, was a clumsy attempt to extend a Yes, a blessing, and I accepted that blessing, offering in return only a nickel a week and my art, my poor little art.
>
> Imitation is praise. Description expresses love. I early arrived at these self-justifying inklings. Having accepted that old Shillington blessing, I have felt free to describe life as accurately as I could, with especial attention to human erosions and betrayals. What small faith I have has given me what artistic courage I have. My theory was that God already knows everything and cannot be shocked. And only truth is useful. Only truth can be built upon. From a higher, inhuman point of view, only truth, however harsh, is holy. The fabricated truth of poetry and fiction makes a shelter in which I feel safe, sheltered within interlaced plausibilities in the image of a real world for which I am not to blame.[53]

This credo is moving, wholly instructive, and contains little with which I disagree. If we believe in God, and examine the real world (which we're not to blame for) and the source in which God reveals its actual makeup and himself, the Scriptures, then indeed we understand nothing can shock him—not the paragraphs of a writer any more than the motives of the person who appears on a university campus or in a high school corridor carrying a firearm.

I'm not sure that means he won't hold the originator of an action responsible for his actions and its results. But rather than assume the role of executor, I'll repeat with emphasis, *From a higher, in-human point of view, only truth, however harsh, is holy.* This is what Scriptures teach, which is why the Bible claims to be, on its self-attesting terms, authoritative and holy; and it is, by the way, exactly what John Calvin iterated: *Anything that contains truth is from God.* No wonder all self-important writers overtly state (or secretly hope) that God is a fairy tale; they otherwise wouldn't receive 100 percent credit for their wonderfully original work.

Here at the conclusion, I'll leave Updike in his Shillington incarnation, staring from his shelter toward the grace of the falling rain, unshakeable in his assurance that he will not die, as I suspect he did not, to his surprise, due to the unconditional nature of the God he championed, for good and for ill, in his writing; or to posit it somewhat in the way of Tolstoy at the conclusion of *The Death of Ivan Ilych*—whether his unshakeable assurance was proved and whether it surprised him or not, we all shall soon find out.

8

Deconstructing God

On Views of Education

Lately America seems not a brave new world, as seekers of the sixties hoped, but a fussy, old-fashioned, exclusive suburb. One can
enter only with an armload of correctness. And no religion, *please*—
mostly meaning no Christianity. And so this residence of exclu-
siveness that is the new America has become, along with politics
of the proper kind, the new religion—America devolving into the
decadence, delirium, and financial chaos of the state-manufactured
standards of Imperial Rome.

Books that appeared over the past decades, beginning with
Allan Bloom's *The Closing of the American Mind*, followed by
Dinesh D'Souza's *An Illiberal Education*, should have provided
sufficient warning. Readers also received reminders from weekly
columns or books by Thomas Sowell; in George M. Marsden's *The
Soul of the American University*, in Stephen M. Carter's *The Culture
of Disbelief*, besides so many books that followed I'll mention only
two of the most recent: *Liberal Fascism*, by Jonah Goldberg, and
One-Party Classroom, by David Horowitz, with Jacob Laksin. The
discerning auditor will note that the above authors represent racial,
ethnic, political, and religious diversity.

Stephen Carter, a professor of law at Yale, notes that Alexis de

Tocqueville, when he visited the young American republic, observed that the "religious atmosphere was the first thing that struck me on arrival in the United States."[1] To Tocqueville, this signified that "liberty was tempered by a common morality," Carter adds. Or, as Tocqueville put it: "Thus, while the law allows the American people to do everything, there are things which religion prevents them from imagining and forbids them to dare."[2]

Not so now, with growing numbers of young people moving from the high per-capita suicide rate of the eighties to drive-by killings and school shootings, in which others seem mere objects, video images in a subjective shooting gallery. "For Tocqueville," Carter writes, "religions provided Americans with the strong moral character without which democracy cannot function; but, perhaps equally important, they helped fill the vast space between the people and the government created in their name—a space, Tocqueville recognized, that the government might otherwise fill by itself."[3]

Carter's book documents the ways in which that space is being filled by federal and state "secular moral judgments" that "trivialize the idea that faith matters to people."[4] Public servants appear reluctant to admit that most Americans (according to polls) would agree with Martin Luther King Jr. when he said that a "just law is a manmade code that squares with the moral law or the law of God."[5] Marsden's crisp and wry book verifies the gradual enshrinement of state-inspired faith, with its increasing hostility to religion, especially Christianity, in the intellectual capitals of America, its universities.

But the most complete and discerning and fair-minded (and therefore hair-raising) book is Warren A. Nord's *Religion and American Education: Rethinking a National Dilemma*, from 1995.[6] In Nord the debate assumes a new level. He is a professor of philosophy at the University of North Carolina, Chapel Hill, not a conservative institution, and a "liberal," as he likely would be labeled, and the premise of his book is that religion must be reinstalled in public education, even at grade and secondary levels, if fairness and equity are to prevail.

What was that?

It sounds as if the liberally educated and generally open-minded intellectuals have at last opened their minds to the semaphore of the Bible-thumpers (as those same intellectuals are inclined to think of them) and have translated their tattoo into a measured voice conveying their sense of disenfranchisement, anguish, and rage. Actually only one intellectual has done this, Warren Nord.

"Secularism is an ideology advocated by secularists, who are opposed to religion and believe that secularization is good,"[7] Nord states, but hastens to add that, to his mind, the secularization of the modern world isn't the *work* of secularists. "Indeed, the secularization of modern civilization was largely unintended,"[8] he states. Tracing the development of different denominations in America, he concludes that religious liberals are, "relatively speaking, optimists. They place a fair amount of confidence in human reason to sort out good and evil, truth and falsehood; hence their openness to traditions other than their own."[9]

So the liberalizing of *religion* in America, to Nord's mind, paved the way for moral secularism. Liberal idealists teaching the humanities, for instance, "channeled into literature emotions that, a half-century earlier, would have been expressed in evangelical Christianity."[10] As a result, the "textbooks, the curriculum, and the governing purposes of education had become almost completely secular by the end of the nineteenth century."[11] And "for public education to be neutral, for it to minimize the extent to which it actively discourages religion, it must take religion seriously as part of the curriculum."[12] Although the Enlightenment had a profound influence on our history, according to Nord, he emphasizes that "there is no way of making sense of American history apart from Christian tradition."[13]

He devotes a hefty chapter to US law, particularly Supreme

Court decisions, in which he registers a cumulative outrage at the ways in which secularism (however it arrived) has been enforced by federal law. The establishment clause of the first article of the Bill of Rights was intended to regulate the federal government, as stated by many eminent forensic minds (all heavily quoted) and was never, in fact, invoked in affairs of the states, in the realm of public education anyway, until the 1940s. So the federal establishment of secular religion, to the exclusion of every other religion, has taken place in public education in the last seventy years. The authorities Nord quotes from before the forties never would have believed a takeover of this magnitude could occur.

The concept of "a wall of separation between church and state" is found in a letter of Thomas Jefferson to a Baptist minister, not in the Bill of Rights or US Constitution, as many seem to believe. The Baptist minister was concerned that Jefferson would install his brand of religion if he was elected president, and Jefferson responded with the remark that he felt a wall of separation should exist between the church and state, not only hoping to garner more votes, but setting the wall between himself (the state) and the church, as the Constitution envisioned.

Given that separatist legal clout, the inevitable usurpation of the daily details of education by the federal government—wrenching it from state and local authority—is the sad text of the remainder of Nord's book. Nature abhors a vacuum, we know, and from the beginning no vacuum existed in public education; its bedrock was religion, from the time of the first Pilgrim and Puritan "public" schools, and, in fact, an overbalance probably existed. Any alternatives, such as Catholic parochial schools, rose in reaction to a religious corner on the market. Public schools in the nineteenth century, says Nord, reflected the majoritarianism of the nation; they were anti-Catholic.

This sentiment was partly installed, via government, by the religious zeal of the public school reformer, Horace Mann, a Unitarian, who wanted his religious views to prevail—not evangelical but exclusively Protestant. Schools in Virginia and elsewhere had been, up until then, Anglican, and in other states had represented local religious convictions. It is interesting to note that while public schools have grown increasingly parochial, if not prejudicial toward religion, there has been an equal and opposite reaction in the sector that was once the most exclusively narrow—private parochial schools.

In *Catholic Schools and the Common Good*, a group of researchers and statisticians, Bryk, Lee, and Holland, set down these changes and the results achieved through them. The formidable bastions of Roman Catholicism are opening their doors to the surrounding community, which often means an inner-city neighborhood. One no longer has to be Catholic or even a believer to attend (which is true of most private Protestant schools) but underpinning the schools is "a vital Catholic social ethic" that provides "a public place for moral norms."[14] The sense of community fostered within the schools, with a cohering center of moral norms, provides a stability that is one of the reasons why parochial school graduates, even when drawn from the inner city, statistically outperform their public school peers. Of equal interest, certainly, is the finding that young women from these schools perceive a greater diversity of career opportunities than their counterparts in public education, although (or is it because?) many of the faculty in the schools are nuns.

Nord summarizes as evenhandedly and thoroughly as one scholar can the multitude of threads of American history that led to the present federal monopoly on public education, so it may be choking on a gnat to say he seems to have missed the auspicious moment that forestalled, anyway for fifty years, government's autocratic hegemony. In February 1926, the US Senate and House held hearings on a proposed Department of Education, before the Senate and House Committees on Education. One of those testifying, J. Gresham Machen, a professor of New Testament at Princeton Seminary, said the proposed goal—uniformity in education—seemed to him not only misguided but "the worst state into which any country can fall."[15]

He stated that "standardization in some spheres is a good thing. It is a good thing in the making of Ford cars; but just because it is a good thing in the making of Ford cars it is a bad thing in the making of human beings."[16] About federal aid to states for education, he said that such "money given . . . always has a string tied to it."[17] This is a truth every American educator has experienced since.

But of greater concern to Machen was the notion that "the children of the State must be educated for the benefit of the State; that idiosyncrasies should be avoided, and the State should devise that method of education which will best promise the welfare of the state."[18] That idea, he pointed out, had its genesis in Plato, and was put into practice, with disastrous results, in Greek states. Then with particular prescience he recognized that the "same principle, of course, appears in practice in other countries in modern times, at its highest development in Germany, in disastrous form in Soviet Russia."[19] That "highest development" was the Austrian School that introduced, via government, its Social Democratic vision into German education ("brownshirts" referred to the official school uniform) with the calamitous results that generations after must indeed never forget. Nor will Russia forget the increasing disaster, following fast after, of Stalin's reign—a yoke once thrown off that seems to be undergoing a refitting for yet another form of serfdom for Russian citizens.

At least one member of the House Education Committee appeared to question the credentials of Machen, a seminary professor, in the realm of public education—as if the idea of "expertise" that so clogs education today was already beginning to suffer, as Neil Postman puts it, a "hardening of the categories." Then the questioner put it to Machen straight: Can he cite an instance when the government interfered, "directly or indirectly, with the operation of any private or church school?"[20] Machen's concern wasn't his own institution, he claimed, and then said, with similar prescience:

"With respect to the future, I do feel, sir, that I am contending for a principle which is absolutely necessary to the principle of religious liberty. There are in the sphere of education tendencies which are directly opposed to religious liberty, such as the effort to produce morality codes [he meant independent institutionally created ones] in the public schools."[21]

The Department of Education didn't appear until the seventies, under the administration of Jimmy Carter, who owed a debt to America's teachers unions, and Nord's research corroborates how, once that department was created, every trend Machen foresaw fell in place. Nord raises the stakes in what I believe is the most important debate engaging America as it enters the twenty-first century—religion in education. Everybody is affected, from the youngest child to the oldest grandparent, including the nation's largest and most ubiquitous and increasingly unionized industry: public education. What Nord is advancing is neither a table- nor Bible-thumping simple answer, but a hope for intellectual conversation about the national dilemma—a let's-sit-down-and-talk-this-through attitude.

It should be helpful to all involved that his concern is for those most intimately affected: children and young adults. In the matter of an institutional code whose precepts were experimented with, *values clarification* (even though its worth was rejected by one of its founders), Nord notes that in any values reached "there is never any careful or systematic appeal to moral or religious thinking and theory."[22] And why should there be? "Too often strict separationism has excluded religion . . . in ways that are not religiously neutral but hostile to religion."[23] Present-day codes and texts advise a student "'to construct the moral universe anew largely by consulting his or her *feelings*'" (emphasis mine).

I've emphasized the last word as a parent who has watched four children during the crisis years (from the age of two until marriage, at least), attempt to construct, from their individual angles of expertise, that sort of universe—in which it's understood that a tantrum has a greater effect than a goodnight kiss—and were unsuccessful I might add, thank God, through their own good sense. Grade and secondary teachers are given a parent's task of dealing with students who haven't acquired the knowledge or the experience necessary for the sorting that underlies all deliberative thought, so that thought of its kind can lead (as adults hope) to an informed, ethical decision.

The rights of students, as the school system installs them, instill a kind of adolescent anarchy. *We will do what I want. You asked me what I think and I told you, and my view is as valid as yours—that's what you said.* This is the undertone of what is taught, and it is post-modernism in toddler's clothes, before students know who Honest Abe is, much less Stanley Fish. A telling example of the result of this attitude is found in "Good Neighbors," a story by Jonathan Franzen in the *New Yorker* Summer Fiction Issue, 2009.[24] The dilemma that was once for philosophers or moral theorists is now our children's: the meaning of meaning. And how can we expect them to sort meaning in a coherent manner (to truncate Nord) without referring to the issues that most Western and Eastern religions have confronted over the ages?

Instead, we equate secularization and scientism—the *doctrine* of science, which is devoid of any moral dimension—with neutrality. But it's not neutral, because "schools must be neutral not just between religions—not favoring Baptists over Episcopalians or Christians over Jews—but they must also be neutral between religion and nonreligion, not favoring religious or secular ways of thinking."[25] Scientism presupposes inherent faith, and some of its apologists have the zeal of tent evangelists, or, in Nord's words: "Science functions as Scripture does in conservative religion, providing unquestioned rules by which all disputes are to be settled."[26]

While some readers may flinch at a few of Nord's assertions, or at his summary descriptions of different denominations at delicate points in their history, he has to be credited for covering the terrain he does (his twenty-three-page bibliography is stunning), in his hope of broadening the conversation between dozens of areas of study and diverse segments of society. Unless religion is taught in school, without dismissive hostility or prejudice at lower levels, and with conviction in advanced college courses, American education will not merely remain at its present impasse, he suggests, but continue to deteriorate, drawing our children and thus society down with it. And presently, only one form of religious politics prevails, as illustrated by David Horowitz in *One-Party Classroom*.

Why should this shock many, as it will, in a country, though post-Tocqueville, where 90 percent of its citizens claim they believe in God, and 70-some percent profess to be Christian? Because of indoctrination, Nord says, as it is delivered in public schools (an entire chapter is devoted to this), in spite of public opinion: a recent Gallup poll indicated that "the great majority of Americans approve of teaching about the major religions of the world (79 percent) and using the Bible in literature, history and social studies classes (75 percent) in public schools."[27] Statistics about the religious makeup of America have been published before, but no volume cross-references the findings in such a number of ways as *One Nation under God: Religion in Contemporary American Society*, by Barry Kosmin and Seymour Lachman.

Nord does not advocate the *practice* of religion in public schools, not at all, nor does he endorse prayer in schools, but: "Parents who take offense at nonsectarian, largely ceremonial graduation prayers should have some small ability to empathize with religious parents whose most basic beliefs and values are rejected over and over again in textbooks and in the curriculum."[28] In a review of texts used at grade, secondary, and college levels (a further study Nord has undertaken), he concluded religion is so rigorously shunned that when it does appear, as in one history text dealing with the settling of America, the effect is often blatant Orwellian disinformation: "Pilgrims are people who make long trips."

He notes that "When the authors [of textbooks] wish to appeal to an authority in resolving some matter, they appeal to psychologists and social scientists, counselors and public opinion surveys."[29] He explains, "My point here is not that this is a *wrong* view of human nature and values, but that it is incompatible with most religious ways of thinking about these things."[30]

Though the majority of Americans say they want religion taught in their schools, they can't be aware of what's going on, or they would see how it's been eviscerated into the nation's remarkable gutless wonder.

The Messianic Character of American Education, by R. J. Rushdoony, documents this exclusion, along with education's religious impulse to *save*. His book seems influential to many that have followed—in the intangible way in which ideas enter the crosscurrents of intellectual table talk. Like Nord, Rushdoony traces the history of education in the US and registers the hardening of its secular purpose, even in the public media, quoting, for instance, from a *New Republic* editorial from 1961 that insists "it is the mission of the state to discourage parochial schools."[31] Some state that would be, a respondent replied; a state that did would surely have institutional schools. Relocating this response, I felt that the influence of the public media is an area that Nord, unlike Postman or McLuhan, has ignored. I mean the propagandizing power of TV.

I encountered *The New Republic*'s suggested form of discouragement in 1980, when, with a dozen other parents, I helped establish a Christian school. My help landed me in court. The laws of North Dakota, the state I was living in at the time, forbade the formation of a school not sanctioned and approved by the state, employing state-appointed teachers, using only curriculum approved by the state, meeting according to state standards; and I was arraigned, along with others, for exercising what I understood was a right. That extreme law has since been rewritten, I'm pleased to report, but its mere existence suggests the depth of the dilemma Nord is addressing.

Few would refute the salubrious effects of a truly liberal education, I hope. But the point Nord keeps emphasizing (and at times he's repetitious) is this: What will the *content* of this education be? If religion is banned, then education has become illiberal; it has, in fact, been discriminatory and needs to be corrected by proper practice, perhaps even by law, though Nord gracefully withdraws from issuing any edicts. He does not favor educational vouchers, given their potential to promote both religious and intellectual segregation, but is afraid they may have to be used, to correct a few of the overwhelming inequities that exist at this crucial point in America's history.

American education has failed in the most basic and essential issue: *Johnny can't think*. The exclusion of religion, meaning the exclusion of a coherent social-moral overview, may be a central cause, Nord suggests. How can you teach not only literature and history and social studies but art and music and law and philosophy, all of which are derived from or informed in the West by the Christian tradition, without admitting the Christian faith exists, or referring to the source many of these writers and composers and visual artists explicitly honor or portray in their work? Much less mention the suppositions in literature and philosophy and law that language and symbols adhere to? Most of these are ethical. How would Native Americans, for instance, respond if any mention of their traditions and religion were banned by law from public schools? As they have responded, I suspect, to compulsory schools set up by the federal government (through denominations) that did indeed commit such banning, in order to "assimilate" them. They've responded with outrage, and rightly so.

The failure of American public education to educate is a statistic even most of its practitioners admit, at least tacitly, as they have for decades. Which profession has the highest percentage of children in private schools? Public school teachers. Dire indicators suggest that nearly half of all high school graduates are illiterate. This, as surely as public education's hostility to religion, has encouraged the home-school movement. The possible dimensions that a parent-guided, self-education can assume, when not corralled by state-sponsored homogenization, is apparent in Theodore Roosevelt, Thomas Edison, and Sylvia Townsend Warner. Edison's mother directed his entire education until she couldn't keep up. No scientist of the time could either, or that person would have come up with Edison's inventions.

Nord's contribution to American education is not a relative matter, but precisely and morally important, and will have a revolutionary impact, I hope, more wide-reaching than Horace Mann's promotion of the "common school" in the 1840s. Because if Nord is not heeded, the effect will be counterrevolutionary, as the books of John Holt were in the sixties and seventies, where his main contention was that all one has to do to teach is to observe the particular child. Parents took note. Indeed, a good many of the sixties' and seventies' generations who aren't on Wall Street or in politics, taught or teach their children at home.

Homegrown education, too, may have its drawbacks, but parents and educators should not accept the red herring offered by those interested in education as a controlling institution: socialization. That brand of getting-along-with-others, when installed and enforced nationally, has the potential to lead, as mentioned, to the leveling barracks attitude that produced the brownshirts of the Third Reich. Youth troops save seals!

Children who can get along with their parents, as even irreligious Freud observed, can get along with anybody. In my travels I tend to deal with all sorts of young people in a variety of situations, and those who are taught at home are invariably more sociable and conversant. It became so apparent I would say to a well-informed one, "Are you homeschooled?"

"Yes, I am."

The answer was not every time given with brio but was in direct contact with me, no glancing or glaring down. Compare this with the slouch and turn-away-with-hands-in-the-pockets of other-educated young people around adults, their heads hanging as if for execution at having to put up with this old-age person, with maybe some toe kicks at the carpet with name-brand running shoes to show how ticked they are that their parents have trotted them out of their room to say hello to this lumbering grunt hog. It can be that bad, as those who presently accuse others of ageism will confirm, along with grandparents who desire only to be friendly.

The graces that children who are taught in the home environment gain are emotional and intellectual and religious freedoms capable of engaging any social milieu. Freedom of that magnitude is what Nord hopes all children in America, through their educational overseers, will regain. And to that I can only add, if I may be granted the latitude, Amen.

9

DYLAN TO CNN

On News and Not News

Serious news arrives in a calamitous context, already upon us, or an artistic one, with its newsworthiness intact. A thousand years before the birth of Jesus, Homer was reciting in verse the lessons and warnings of war and, in contrast, extolling domestic life on home ground.

The troubadour poets of southern France and northern Spain and Italy were nobles who held political strongholds from the twelfth to the fourteenth centuries. They were news-bringers, and Richard I of England was one of them. Troubadours employed servants, called jongleurs, to set their words to music, so it arrived in the context of what one might call "artistic news."

In England, troubadours were named minstrels, from the Latin *minister*, meaning "servant." The poems of troubadours are preserved in the canon of Anglo-Saxon and Provençal poetry, so you may wonder if their role as news-bringers, as the anchors of their day, is accurate. It was only their lasting compositions that survive, I suspect, because the fate of their more pointed compositions is clear from their end: "The great cause of the decadence and ruin of the troubadours," a trustworthy version of the *Britannica*, the 14th edition (of 1929) states, "was the struggle between Rome and the heretics."

The minstrels of England didn't fare much better. They sank to the level of forming a guild in London, a kind of union that all were supposed to join, but didn't, of course, since they were writers. Finally minstrels faced the troubadours' fate; the Church denounced them, and "The state also viewed them with disfavor as men who wasted their own time and that of their listeners. For these masterless men carried the news from place to place, sang biting lampoons against unpopular ministers, or voiced the wrongs of the poor. . . . Local riots seem to have owed much to their activity." They were put in stocks, whipped, imprisoned.

Why "a trustworthy version" of the *Britannica*? Because in our time facts have been fiddled with or details left out, as most realize. This descent into "newspeak," as George Orwell called it, or "spin" as we say, has picked up such speed that what we take as facts, even those of history, are often forgeries. Big Brother was in operation long before 1984, giving his version of events, but we were too busy with TV, that mind-numbing nurse and anesthetist of his, to notice.

I'm beginning to feel I'm:

> Knock, knock, knockin' on heaven's door,
> Knock, knock, knockin' on heaven's door.[1]

One brief book holds most of the actual records gathered over the centuries on the life of Shakespeare, while it would probably take a library to hold all the books and ephemera poured out on the details of the life of the phenomenon known as Bob Dylan. I heard his first album in 1963 when he was my age, twenty-one, just a kid (though at the time I thought I was getting on in age), and was drawn so far in I never quite found a way out. He was delivering to my generation not only political and cultural news but, with each album, was clearly charting an individual spiritual odyssey—his own.

He came from the North Country, across my native state, where the wind hits heavy on the borderline—Hibbing, Minnesota, at the edge of the Mesabi Range. Excavations for iron ore open up outside Hibbing in a pit leagues deep and miles wide. The first sound of his voice entered me like electricity. I didn't think of him as a great poet, as academics have, but a troubadour, a news-bringer in touch with his and the world's makeup and not about to falsify his report for any favored political group or audience.

When I think of the first album I heard, *The Freewheelin' Bob Dylan*, I'm astonished at how the songs—"Masters of War," "Blowin' in the Wind," "A Hard Rain's A-Gonna Fall" and the rest—seem written down the raw nerve of my generation. The effect was a rage of recognition. We were displaced and restless and knew something was amiss but didn't have the words for it. The blame for our condition is usually laid on the repressive nature of the Eisenhower years, but I won't repeat that rhetoric. The decade was partly a comfort in the placid way it passed under aging Ike. America has never again had quite the same confidence. There was a tenderness to the time, too, expressed in the closeness of families, which may have risen from the knowledge that all that you cherished could disappear in a flash—a literal one.

Every week we heard from schoolteachers or radio prophets or newsreels a new twist on the atomic bomb, now the *hydrogen* bomb. Once a month or so in my grade school we had a drill in which we practiced leaping under our desks or against a wall, away from windows, to avoid the blast of the flash that could crisp us like the bodies in the film footage from Hiroshima and Nagasaki. We saw these and learned what to expect and how to react, so I sometimes think we were inarticulate from a numbed state of shock.

And then there was Dylan. These were the words we were searching for, an outpouring of them from this quirky writer and musician who took his name from the last Romantic poet, Dylan Thomas (no matter what he may have later said), though his adopted father was Woody Guthrie, a radical populist—Dylan from the northern hotbox of LaFollette and the Nonpartisan League. He delighted in all he did—laughing and making mistakes on records and leaving this on the tracks, happy to take his act anywhere he was asked.

"The Times They are A-Changin'," he told us, and we were "Only a Pawn in Their Game," those "Masters of War," but he promised we would see a day "When the Ship Comes In."

> Oh the foes will rise
> With the sleep still in their eyes . . .
> Then they'll raise their hands,
> Sayin' we'll meet all your demands,
> But we'll shout from the bow your days are numbered.
> And like Pharaoh's tribe,
> They'll be drownded in the tide,
> And like Goliath, they'll be conquered.[2]

This is the original of what contemporary Christians call a ministry of music. Before this we had gospel singers and country singers who added gospel to their repertoire, but none was reaching to a specific audience with religious imagery and content. Killjoys said about Dylan, "Aw, he can't sing," or "He can't play," as if that dismissed him.

He set the agenda for a generation and neither it nor the world has recovered. He galvanized our view on civil rights: integration, Selma, and Oxford. His songs sent thousands to picket lines. He wrote such an articulate series of antiwar songs that he can ultimately be seen, with his voice and lyrics, as the one who ended the war in Vietnam. His words drew protesters by the ten thousands.

He didn't write the slogan for the generation—"Don't trust anybody over thirty"—but his songs inspired it. They were pitiless in describing the "generation gap," as it came to be called—"Because something is happening here / But you don't know what it is / Do you, Mr. Jones?"[3] He made drugs appear a tool and prohibition of elderly folk ("Everybody must get stoned!"[4]) and exuded a casual attitude toward sex ("Don't think twice, it's all right"[5]) yet sang with a heart-stopping tenderness about women, beginning with the

"Girl from the North Country" to "Oh, Sister," and beyond. He added another theme—"Make love, not war"—to the agenda of those now called "hippies," who before were socialists or utopians or commies or beatniks.

Whether we agree with him or take exception at every point, there's no denying his impact—in those days before the Beatles or Stones or all their current imitators. This is the news of real history. In a matter of years, so that it seemed to happen overnight, the repressive view of the body and its sexuality, present in the Christian and most every contemporary community, swung to the other side—sexual license. This may have been due to one aspect of the Eisenhowerish sense of community, where many in my generation, as they grew up, heard from their parents not so much about a moral or ethical standard as fearful considerations of what the neighbors might think.

In 1965, at the Newport Festival, a host of followers booed Dylan off the stage because he introduced into his act the instruments we associate with rock, even "Christian" rock. Before, he had accompanied himself on his acoustic guitar and harmonica. His admirers and felt he had deserted them and the cause.

He wasn't a chameleon; he was maturing, the enduring quality of a news-bringer. He didn't see himself as a celebrity or an artiste (he sang about these with irony or scorn) or the tool of any cause, but as a performer who was out to do as much of the best as one can. Christians still seem confused on this point; singing is a ministry, according to the contemporary idiom, when it is more properly a vocation chosen because of obvious gifts.

The glory of Dylan is the record of his spiritual journey. That journey became more readily apparent in the album *John Wesley Harding*, stepped up in *New Morning*, and was made manifest in *Slow Train Coming*, *Shot of Love*, and the album with a title so specific it's hard to miss, *Saved*.

I was blinded by the devil
Born already ruined,
Stone-cold dead
As I stepped out of the womb
By His grace I have been touched,
By His word I have been healed,
By His hand I've been delivered,
By His spirit I've been sealed
I've been saved
By the blood of the lamb.[6]

You can hardly get more explicit, and here is the genesis of Christian rock and all its groups and groupies. As Dylan was the musical father of Bruce Springsteen and dozens like him, so he was of Rich Mullins and that wave. He brought raucous art to gospel music, the cymbal-clanging clangor of the Psalms. When he stopped singing openly about salvation, a new set of followers abandoned him, claiming he was no longer "Christian."

I'm not his apologist (think, though, of the license and backsliding we tolerate in ourselves) but I suspect he found the liberty of serving his Savior in his art rather than always assuming a churchy confession. This may be a loss to those who found faith through him, but his end is the celebration of God in the discipline and art of song and the good news true art can bring.

His first identity, as a folk singer, defines his work. He wrote for the folk, as Shakespeare did—and here I do not equate the quality of their art but outlook. Most of those at a Shakespeare play were poor, called groundlings; they stood or sat on the ground. The stage of Shakespeare's day, developed from the open courts of inns, was built to accommodate them. In 1599, Shakespeare, now prosperous, put together with others a playhouse across the Thames, in Southwark, named the Globe.

Its shape was a wooden O, with a stage extending into its interior, open to the sky. An inner wall formed a kind of cloister that surrounded the stage, roofed with thatch, on two levels. Lords and the ladies and some Puritans who didn't wish to be seen at a play sat here, somewhat as in a baseball stadium. The diamond would be the stage, much reduced, since the Globe was only eighty feet in diameter.

Groundlings gathered like groupies at a rock festival; you get the picture if you've seen a concert in a stadium. They were in intimate proximity to the actors, and the presence of flesh-and-blood performers always undoes the shadowy never-never land of movies and TV. Those media, because of the frame they use, tend to open a window to the Peeping Tom in us. The assumption of their scenes is: Hey, you voyeur, gaze on! They entice us to buy into the distancing destructiveness of another medium: pornography.

Dylan was never accused of obscenity onstage. Sometimes he was rambling or seemed to have had too much of something and you never knew how the songs you held in your memory might come out. But he always went from beginning to end, a professional dramatist. His act was artful, from the simplicity of the early ones—onstage alone with a stool and guitar and his harmonica in its holder at his mouth—to the arranged tours with a theme, such as "The Rolling Thunder Review." Dylan writes of fools and clowns but doesn't assume he's Shakespeare, though Shakespeare too wrote songs. He was as popular in his day as Dylan in his heyday. We should be able to see in both a relevant truth: to reach great numbers you don't have to ratchet the level of art down to the lowest denominator. Dylan and Shakespeare seemed always to have between their ears the best advice I've heard: you have to assume your reader is at least as bright as you.

Dylan's songs do not discriminate, as the best writing does not. Sometimes it may seem he's delivering messages from another planet; in fact, a favorite album of mine is *Planet Waves*. It's about love for a wife and children, so we come to understand that the planet that animates him is none other than Earth. He was celebrating domestic life on home ground. He sang with eloquence about so many issues at a time when the news about them was needed, and has so often hit the target dead center, I often wonder if he isn't hot-wired to a manifestation of the Holy Ghost.

The premise of television news is that we're dumb and dumber, as a movie put it. The obscenity in this is its disdain for humankind. This is epitomized in the bland and repetitive disclosures and outright deception of CNN, which some first called Chicken Noodle Network, for its hodgepodge of slippery stuff. CNN was legally caught in a deception a while ago, but the deception goes on daily in their selection of "news," not to mention the engulfing commentary. There is art in this, or anyway artfulness, as in the engulfing gulf wars, which had the appearance on CNN of a miniseries from Hollywood. The deception in this was supreme, since thousands were being killed, women and children, more than in Bosnia, but our viewpoint was CNN's: aerial glitz; bombs homing in on windows of buildings, not burning babies.

Ted Turner, the guru of CNN, has stated his contempt for a certain class of people, summed up in a word he uses about them: stupid. He means Christians. CBS and NBC and ABC aren't quite as forthcoming, but their view is the same, judging from content. Christians seem a convenient target for the networks' contempt of the audience in general, and perhaps this is deserved, since they keep watching.

And not only keep watching but click to programs with scenes and words more provocative than in any novel. About the hard copy of art, they agitate to have it banned, and then sink into the hypnotizing fuzz of TV. There they see people of faith or with any ethical standard detonated by the likes of Oprah and Chris Matthews—the only slice of society it's safe to slam, even on the worst shows shot through with canned laughter to cover their emptiness. No wonder books on self-esteem sell at such a clip to Christians.

People of faith, especially those who confess to take Jesus seriously, have to start looking away from TV for the news and stop imbibing as fact what they take in from Tom Brokaw or the latest anchor on CNN. They receive this as if a prophet of the Bible were speaking, and sometimes seem to believe it as much as Scripture itself. The sad news is this: the *they* is us. And if we don't soon call a halt to this, we face the prospect of being clicked off, shut away from the artists and artisans and jongleurs and minstrels who are delivering the good news within the grace and health of a responsible relationship, and will be no better off than specks of light going dim and then snapping away into the black hole of our universe inside the tube.

The Faith of Shakespeare

On My Favorite Actor

GLANCING AT THE AMBIENCE

Shakespeare seems to undergo a revival every decade or two, his inexhaustible corpus tottering onstage to be revealed as yet another fashionable young man (or woman) in tights. And so in 2009, Jude Law, a British Hollywood import, was busy in a run of *Hamlet* on Broadway while King Lear's daughters attempted to second-guess what they had done in *The Tragedy of King Lear*—a disquieting, post-mod variant of the *Rosencrantz and Guildenstern Are Dead* variety—besides a superb production of *The Tempest*.

The genesis of the present revival, whose run has been longer than most, dates to the Mel Gibson film—not *The Passion of the Christ* but *Hamlet*—though scholars and critics were busy with Shakespeare before Hollywood saw he was a literary type who could spin a good yarn and might deserve a remake. Gibson's durably performed Hamlet was truncated to emphasize a Thomas Kyd theme: revenge—a source of joy to the young, especially when directed against one's parent—and at the same time a Hollywood jack-of-several-trades, Sam Wannamaker, began a reconstruction of the Globe Theater, the venue of many of Shakespeare's successes, at its approximate original site, until Brit law balked at the American intrusion and construction was halted and then picked up, under another auspices, two years later.

Branaugh soon appeared as a starstruck warrior exuding the celestial dimension that royalty of ultimate prerogative used to enjoy, warring in this case against kingdom divisions in his *Henry V.* In *Much Ado About Nothing*, he conjured a magic musicality for the Hollywood screen that far exceeds Broadway's shouting bravado stitched with filigree; and followed that with a robber baron Iago, teeth clenched in fomenting evil. And then in a conclusion that seemed inevitable, he produced and directed and starred in *Hamlet*, an uncut four-hour film, into which he poured what seemed personal woes—slo-mo redeemed by Claudius, Horatio, and batty Robin Williams—with little connection to the glory of the celestial that studs the text of *Hamlet* with an omnipresence like stars.

The Royal Shakespeare Company (RSC) began issuing videos of its productions, and a mod *Romeo + Juliet* arrived like an import from the *Titanic*. And finally the growing following got an intuitive and not unkindly cut of the fellow himself, in *Shakespeare in Love.* Academy Awards to Will! And on and on, so many new Shakespeare films that Anthony Lane in an issue of the *New Yorker* of the late nineties had a long feature article entitled "Tights! Camera! Action!"[1]

The momentum of the latest revival has built, at least partly due to the Hollywood connection, until it seems producers of films and BBC specials and picture books (and picture books of BBC specials, such as Michael Wood's *Shakespeare*) will never rest, yet never quite displace the primary players of the verbal O, the scholars. Their outpouring forms a widening stream as journals and quarterlies and books keep up a tumble into the present, redefining and perfecting the elusive fellow we know as Shakespeare. Even those who aren't exactly interested in him but don't want to appear retro will drop the name of this ancient who wrote sonnets and such.

With this kind of cultural current strumming through us nearly daily, another force rose to the fore: the anti-Stratfordians, formerly called the Baconians. They are usually journalists or psychologists or social commentators who came on the corpus late and like to light into others who pretend Shakespeare is Shakespeare when actually he is, well, Bacon or Ben Jonson or de Vere of Oxford or maybe even Kit Marlowe. Their ranks run the gamut from George Bernard Shaw, who disputed almost everything, to Joe Sobran.

Anti-adherents, like bloodhounds, catch any scent of interest in the aging ancient and so, in 1991, after the Gibson *Hamlet*, the *Atlantic* ran a cover story pitting Edward de Vere, Earl of Oxford, against the rustic Dogberry known as Shakespeare.[2] *Harper's*, in 1999, did a cover story, "Who Was Shakespeare?" and the anti-Stratfordians have their backtrackings and screeds sprinkled through the outpour of all the arriving books.[3] Their attitude and outlook is summed up by David Mamet, the actor, playwright, screenwriter, and director (a variety of roles familiar to Shakespeare) in his *Three Uses of the Knife*:

> The anti-Stratfordians hold that Shakespeare didn't write Shakespeare's plays—it was another fellow of the same name, or of a different name. In this they invert the meglomaniacal equation and make themselves not the elect, but the *superior* of the elect. Barred from composing Shakespeare's plays by a regrettable temporal accident, they, in the fantasy of most every editor, accept the mantle of *primum mobile*, consign the (falsely named) creator to oblivion, and turn to the adulation of the crowd for their deed of discovery and insight—so much more thoughtful and intellectual than the necessarily sloppy work of the writer.[4]

Their view is really a reversion to the highly developed class or caste system of England in Tudor times, when it was assumed that only a person of noble birth, from a select society, an aristocrat of superior breeding and race, possessed sufficient intelligence to compose a masterpiece. Anybody from a rural setting was a dolt, likely a redneck (a condition gained from bending to hoe weeds)—a view smuggled into the present by post-mod litterateurs from the literary-political stronghold of New York, if not Minneapolis, in its own eyes the defining ground of literature. The anti-Stratfordians seem to want to place a foot on the throat of Shakespeare and arrange themselves as set pieces in the foreground, an action worthy of a Shakespeare play on the greenest of envies.

In a kind of deference to the naysayers, and to save space, I refer to him as WS, taking the lead of Anthony Burgess in his sixties novel, *Nothing Like the Sun*. Too many variations on his name, often in his own hand, exist to pinpoint WS's exact preferred spelling, and it helps to know that English was in the midst of a sea change in his era, its shifting mutations reaching our present state, and he seems to have used the vowels and consonants, the ones that made up his own name, even, that to him felt right.

THOSE GREENE ENVIES

Hemmings and Condell, fellow actors and managers with the one you recognized as WS, got together to gather up his plays after he died and mentioned in their introduction that he "wrote with hardly a blot." Ben Jonson repeated their remark in his journal and said would WS had blotted far more!—less matter with better art—still greenly jealous of dead WS. In Shakespeare's will, as it is known to scholars and the keepers of Britain's National Archives, WS leaves memorial rings to Hemmings and Condell, among others; and leaves the family's second-best bed to his wife, presumably because she inherited it from her father and wanted it back. Hemmings and Condell are also mentioned, along with a *W Shakespeare*, in the court records of Elizabeth I and James I, as members of a company called The Lord Chamberlain's Men—later altered, in honor of the odd new monarch from Scotland, to The King's Men.

It would be difficult to deceive two royal courts, replete with influential hangers-on and backroom gossips, or to delude the Lord Chamberlain, responsible for all entertainments held in Britain—centuries before the KGB or CIA—about a person called "Shakespeare." The two monarchs named above commissioned plays by him, Elizabeth requesting a reappearance of Falstaff, thus *The Merry Wives of Windsor*, and these plays were performed by his companies.

Before any of the plays were known to a larger public, the writer Robert Greene referred to him as the "Johannes Factotum" or jack of all trades of the profession, a person monopolizing the business—actor, theater manager, playwright—"the upstart crow, beautified by *our* feathers" (my italics), a rewording of a line from one of WS's early *Henry VI* sequences.[5] Greene's meaning was that WS was rewriting or collaborating on the plays of others, as a theater manager of his day commonly did, and producing beauties better than the originals, inciting the envy of Greene and other playwrights, a condition that might have led to *Othello*.

Robert Frost, the rare American poet who wanted to write blank verse as subtle and complex as WS, and whose poems lean toward the dramatic, either internally or in the form of dialogues or mini-dramas or masques, said, "I look at a poem as a performance. I look on the poet as a man of prowess, just like an athlete. He's a performer."[6] He also notes that "probably way back somewhere" somebody noted that poetry is "the marrow of wit. There's got to be wit."[7]

About Bacon we can say that wit in him is conjured from a kind of academic eloquence—he smells of the closet of ratiocination or the closeted lawyer-philosopher he was—and seems so caught up for most of his career petitioning or lobbying the court to install him as chief legal counsel, a position his father held, he completed only two of the six volumes of philosophy he intended to write, while WS, even when immersed in tragedy, includes the balancing agenbite of inwit, in thirty-plus plays.

Why bother with this, one might wonder, and indeed one would not, one would summarily dismiss the anti-Stratfordians if it weren't that they acquired so much steam in 1916, for instance, that George Fabyan, a menagerie keeper, brought a suit calling WS "a faker"—Francis Bacon wrote the plays, he said—and filed a court injunction to cancel the Tercentenary (three-hundred-year) celebration of Shakespeare's birth.

Once again, it was Hollywood, in the form of the film producer Richard Selig, who came to the rescue. Selig appeared before Judge Richard S. Tuthill of the Circuit Court of Chicago, where Fabyan's complaint originated, and

> asked that Fabyan be enjoined from defaming Shakespeare. Injunction granted. Fabyan vowed to take his case to the Supreme Court. . . . On May 6 it was reported in the *Mirror* that Judge Tuthill had studied all the evidence and lifted the injunction, having concluded that Bacon *did* write the plays. On May 13, the *Mirror* reported that Judge Tuthill had overruled his own decision, and awarded the plays to Shakespeare after all.

The *Mirror* then states, "The Shakespeare Tercentenary may now proceed uninhibited."[8]

This report is by Dr. Charles Shattuck, in the summation to his *Shakespeare on the American Stage* (Vol. 2), published by the Folger Library in 1987. At an earlier date the interest in WS had sunk to such a low ebb Dr. Shattuck said he could not, out of thirty-six thousand students attending the University of Illinois, enlist enough enrollees to justify teaching the undergraduate course that was so popular I heard about it soon after I arrived on campus, and sat in on one semester with seventy-five others. It was this survey class that was canceled due to insufficient enrollment.

We might well leave the dust of this there, or back at the turn of the century, if it weren't that the *Atlantic* and *Harper's* and other interests reignite the controversy at varying intervals. This is the way that Harold Bloom, in a part of his contribution to the *Harper's* cover story, claims he continued to teach WS through that slack seventies period in American academic history:

> The academy, as everyone knows, is shot to pieces. Even at Yale, I am surrounded by courses in gender and power, transsexuality and queer theory, multiculturalism, and all the other splendors that now displace Chaucer, Milton, Shakespeare, and Dickens.

But the worst may well be over. A decade ago [when Dr. Shattuck couldn't garner one undergrad class], I would introduce my Graduate Shakespeare seminar (never my Undergraduate [perhaps Bloom couldn't garner one either]) by solemnly assuring the somewhat resentful students that *all* of Shakespeare, and not just the Sonnets, had been written by Lucy Negro, Elizabethan England's most celebrated East Indian whore. Anthony Burgess in his splendid fictive life, *Nothing Like the Sun*, [way ahead of Hollywood, in 1964] had identified Lucy Negro as the Dark Lady of the Sonnets, and thus Shakespeare's peerless erotic catastrophe, resulting in heartbreak, venereal disease, and relatively early demise. Stone-faced (as best I could), I assured my graduate students that all their anxieties were to be set aside, since the lustful and brilliant Lucy Negro actually had composed the plays and Sonnets. Thus they could abandon their political reservations and read "Shakespeare" with assured correctness, since Lucy Negro was, by definition, multicultural, feminist, and post-colonial. And also, I told them, we could set aside the covens of Oxfordians, Marlovians, and Baconians in the name of the defrauded Lucy Negro.[9]

If nothing other rose out of the recent revival than Bloom's *Shakespeare: The Invention of the Human*, it was worth the *deus ex machina* of Hollywood for that. Bloom views WS as a nonpareil, the measure of literature since, which is quite a plateful, since Bloom is America's premier professional reader, perhaps the best read person alive, not to mention his acuity, his charm, and the unfazed way in which he looks to the rock bottom of a book without hauling in a shipload of critical superstructure to render him superior to the text. I suspect, however, that few doubt how often he *is* superior to it.

His contention is that Hamlet and Falstaff are written-out or literary representations of the heights and depths a human being is capable of, as we understand humankind down to the present. The thought feels agreeably Platonic, as filtered through Aquino-Thomists, but Bloom, mild as a March pasqueflower, believes the parameters of our species were forged by WS, and have not been superseded since. I am ready to second that, and will add that most observations in Bloom's 745-page thunking tome are artfully woven and arranged:

> But that is typical of Hamlet's consciousness, for the prince has a mind so powerful that the most contrary attitudes, values, and judgments can coexist within it coherently, so coherently indeed that Hamlet nearly has become all things to all men, and to some women. Hamlet incarnates the value of personality, while turning aside from the value of love. If Hamlet is his own Falstaff (Harold Goddard's fine formulation), he is a Falstaff who doesn't need Hal, any more than he needs poor Ophelia, or even Horatio, except as a survivor who will tell the prince's story. The common element in Falstaff's ludic mastery and in Hamlet's dramaturgy is the employment of great wit as a counter-Machiavel, as a defense against a corrupted world.[10]

AN ANTI-BLOOM COBBLEATURE

Well, yes, yet there is a point at which I resist, if I may, Bloom's insistence on "Hamlet As Nihilist" (Part VII, first chapter).[11] Hamlet indeed loves Horatio, while Bloom suggests he merely uses him, or else Hamlet wouldn't take him into his confidence (III ii 53-72), and Horatio loves Hamlet as an adoring younger brother.

A charitable look at a contrasting view is available in a book I came across in an Oxford bookstore. The author is George Morrison, MA, DD, who explains its genesis in his preface: "The following pages embody the notes which I used for a series of addresses given in Wellington Church, Glasgow, on Sunday nights at the close of the evening service. The very large attendance, and the keen and unfailing interest displayed, have led me to publish them, in the hope that they may prove helpful to others."[12] That is half the preface. The remainder is a bow to textual scholars— "those masters of criticism and exposition at whose feet I have sat in discipleship since my college days"[13]—and how Morris "deliberately confined myself to a few of the greater plays which one might assume to be familiar to an audience gathered from all classes of the community."[14]

The class structure was more apparent in the portion of Britain lying below Glasgow, the birthplace and continual habitation (as far as we know) of WS, that is, England.

However fortune delivered the book to me, I opened it (as now, at random, its insight apparent at every turn), and read:

> Lady Macbeth, whatever she may be, is not an utterly callous woman. A careful reading of the play makes that evident. She has to pray to be unsexed (I, v, 42); she needs wine to make her bold (II, ii, 1); she cannot slay Duncan for he is like her father (II, ii, 12-14); after the murder she cannot bear the darkness (V, i, 25-27). And the awful revelation of her sleep-walking [the blood she tries to wash from her hands] betrays a nature different in the deeps from that of an utterly heartless, callous woman.
>
> She was a woman of an indomitable will, who never let "I dare not" wait upon "I would." She has far less imagination than her husband, for Macbeth was of "imagination all compact" [MND, V.i.8] She saw intensely but not imaginatively; she thought that "a little water" would put all things right (II, ii, 67); she failed to picture the remorse and agony that would cause bloodstains to burn like fire.[15]

The book is entitled *Christ in Shakespeare*, and in conclusion to this portion of his talk on *Macbeth*, Morrison notes how Macbeth is tempted "from without not only by malignant powers of darkness; he is tempted also by his dearest.

"So was Jesus tempted by Simon Peter. So is many a man tempted. It has been said that when the devil wants to snare an Englishman he generally does it through his wife and children."[16]

The book was published in 1928 (assuming the dated preface signifies its year of publication) and registers the understanding of a parish pastor in Great Britain at the time—which suggests that Morrison's book is relevant to us, too, although most Americans assume our separation from England included a break from the strictures of social class that immigrants hoped to escape. Not so. I will return to this.

BACK TO BLOOMERY

To take somewhat the tack of Morrison, in response to Bloom's characterization of Hamlet as a nihilist, I find in many of Hamlet's speeches a Christian outlook, a foreboding from the very start:

> Or that the Everlasting had not fixed
> His canon 'gainst self-slaughter! Oh, God! God!
>
> (I, i)

an idea alien to a rational nihilist, as the next is not:

> How weary, stale, flat, and unprofitable
> Seem to me all the uses of this world!
> Fie on it! Ah, Fie! 'Tis an unweeded garden
> That grows to seed, things rank and gross in nature
> Possess it merely. That it should come to this!
>
> (I, ii, 133–137)

though a good metaphor for the world. Hamlet's reflexive response to his father's appearance as a ghost is

> Angels and ministers of grace defend us!
>
> (I, iv, 39)

And when he contemplates the same moment somewhat later—

> . . . The Spirit that I have seen
> May be the Devil, and the Devil hath power
> To assume a pleasing shape. Yea, and perhaps
> Out of my weakness and my melancholy,
> As he is very potent with such spirits,
> Abuses me to damn me.
>
> (II, ii, 627–632)

See his speech to the players (II, ii, 305–321) or the best-known soliloquy, at high tide of the play, when he breaks off his contemplation on suicide, the logical conclusion for a true nihilist who wants to exit the nada world of nothingness, to say,

—perchance to dream. Aye, there's the rub,
For in that sleep of death what dreams may come
When we have shuffled off this mortal coil
Must give us pause. There's the respect
That makes calamity of so long life.

(III, i, 65–69)

"Sleep," a new covenant designation for death, reminds us how Hamlet exclaims, "Oh, God, I could be bounded in a nutshell and count myself a king of infinite space, were it not that I have bad dreams!"

No need to follow this further but simply to note that at the turning point of the play, when Hamlet starts to draw his sword to kill Claudius, he thinks,

Now might I do it pat, now he is praying,
And now I'll do it. And so he goes to Heaven,
And so I am revenged. That would be scanned:
A villain kills my father, and for that
I, his sole son, do this same villain send
To Heaven.
Oh, this is hire and salary, not revenge.

(III, iii, 73–79)

He would become the Devil's salaried emissary, saving from damnation the one he hopes to damn by execution, and from that moment the play revolves from the pivot of "Heaven," circled by the silence of that absent line. Christian scruples thwart his promise of revenge. In the end he pays, like Macbeth, less for his inability to wreak revenge than for his hapless drive toward murder (WS's twist on "revenge plays"), dispatching his culture-attuned school chums along the way, harried by the one who has power to assume not only a pleasing shape but the habiliments of his father, added to the pride in his own dueling abilities. Notice all the references to the Devil and hell and purgatory in the play, as Stephen Greenblatt does in *Hamlet in Purgatory*, and Hamlet's statement that he defies augury, with his following Christian resignation (IV, ii, 217–22).

THE ACTOR I ADORE

Assuming an actor to be the author WS, or vice versa, many instances suggest such an authorship. He alludes to the theater in nearly every play with a sense of authority, actor and theater manager that he was. His was the dyer's hand, so stained with the profession it didn't seem odd to him to have the central character of one of his better known plays, rather than enter into the soul searching that tragic characters often undergo in their downhill slide, say instead, "Life's but a walking shadow, a poor player / That struts and frets his hour upon the stage / And then is heard no more."

Or the ubiquitous prince about to give a group of actors a scene that will eventually bring his own death down on him: "Speak the speech, I pray you, as I pronounced it to you, trippingly on the tongue. . . ."

"Oh, God, I could be bounded in a nutshell"—Hamlet now taking on an actor's role—"I could be bounded in a nutshell and count myself a king of infinite space"—and then he crosses the bridge already mentioned—"were it not that I have bad dreams."

"The play's the thing wherein I'll catch the conscience of the king!" he says, and of the actor who will play the lead in the play within the play with lines he's written, he wonders what the actor would do "had he the motive and the cue for passion that I have."

The motive and the "cue," an actor's *sine qua non*, make up the lifeblood of a role, denoting the reasons for a character's actions—every cue prompts him to enter or speak his next speech. These definitions aren't of importance to a courtier philosopher, but necessary to the theater and can be found not only in the plays but also the Sonnets of WS, as in these examples from several sources:[17]

> Had you not come upon your cue, my lord—*Richard III*
> Now we speak upon our cue, and our voice is imperial—*Henry V*
> The clock gives me my cue—*Merry Wives of Windsor*
> 'Deceiving me' is Thisby's cue; she is to enter now—*MND*
> As an unperfect actor on the stage—*Sonnet 23*

> Were it my cue to fight, I should have known it
> Without a prompter—*Othello*

The prompter here snares down the theater world. But yet one more, from *Richard II*:

> As in a theater, the eyes of men,
> After a well-graced actor leaves the stage,
> Are idly bent on him who enters next,
> Thinking his prattle to be tedious:
> Even so, or with much more contempt, men's eyes
> Did scowl on gentle Richard.

The inter-threaded nature of these references, scattered through the plays in a pattern like lace, draw tighter the further one reads in WS. A legend of his early career is that he was a hostler at a theater, a predecessor to the car valet, the person who took your mount or team and carriage to a hitching place while you attended a play—one of his many suggested apprenticeships. Other scholars suspect he was a tutor for a wealthy family, or joined Lord Strange's troupe when it passed through his territory, and was later clerk to a lawyer. None of this can be confirmed, and that period is termed "the lost years." But whatever else the author of the plays attributed to WS might have been up to, it's clear from the plays themselves that he kept sharpening his skills as an actor.

JUICY OR JUDICIOUS USE OF BIOGRAPHY

It helps to have some insight into the life of Shakespeare, as much as one can, to recognize the role of religion (and at times the evasion of churchgoing) in the life of WS. The British biographer Park Honan delivers on this score, and he is the rare scholar whose humility renders his scholarship resonant. When he entered grad school, he told his supervisor he intended to write a biography of WS; before the supervisor "sent me on to my friend Paul Turner, James Sutherland told me, over sherry, to look into other writers 'first.'"[18]

During his academic term Honan wrote biographies of

Browning, Arnold, and Austen (later Marlowe, less satisfactory), keeping up the research for his work on WS, and when he was a professor emeritus, finally published the biography he first envisioned as an ambitious graduate student in postwar (WW II) London, *Shakespeare: A Life.*

The wait was worth it. Honan's *Life* stands above the tide of numberless others, not only in the way it builds on recorded history recently exhumed—as by S. Schoenbaum in his chronicling of every shred of documentation, legal and otherwise, that exists on WS[19]—but equally in Honan's gentle dispelling of anecdotal and unproved myths and legends. Many of these were formed in a forty-page sketch by Nicholas Rowe, written in 1709, almost a full century after the death of WS, and taken as certitude for centuries.

Honan knows Ivor Brown, E. K. Chambers, G. Wilson Knight, A. L. Rowse, Dover Wilson, M. C. Bradbrooks, Frank Kermode (whose recent *The Age of Shakespeare* buttresses many of Honan's findings but is, to my taste, rather flatfooted), and the bulk of the more traditional crowd, besides the nay-saying anti-Stratfordians who raise or have raised their voices in anguish. Honan unearths a variety of sources that document the historical era into which WS was born, the matrix of his surround, so it becomes clear that x and x could not have occurred, because the potential for such an event did not exist at the time, or it is clear that WS experienced x and x, because it was the experience of all Tudor youth in the rigid society of the era—and Honan is a trustworthy scholar, not a sniper at jots and tittles.

His prose is compressed, direct, uncluttered, with a tug to it of wrapping the right words within a telling phrase, and it registers a sifting acuity that lifts each passage into the realm of accuracy—a book of such precision I enjoyed it for two years before I finally finished, due to the angles of thought even a paragraph had the power to carry me off into.

James Shapiro's later book, *1599*, covering one year in the life of WS, is of similar quality, especially when it enters textual exegesis on the complicated weaving of contemporary politics and religion in WS. The way in which Shapiro locates these crossroads in *Julius Caesar* is absolutely brilliant; there's no other word for it. Shapiro may have spent too many years in comfort in the ivory tower, however, due to a few everyday commonsense errors, when he asserts, for instance, that "anti-freeze" was used in the foundation of the original Globe, to keep the mortar from setting up when actual antifreeze, not available in 1599, is a petroleum product that would turn mortar to an oily disaster, and he probably means some form of salt, such as calcium chloride. He also makes a to-do over the *large amount* of malted barley WS kept hidden—eighty bushels, which isn't enough to fill a pickup box, so not such a great amount, actually.

A glimpse of the actual history leading to the Renaissance and therefore WS was laid down by W. H. Auden in his introduction to *Medieval and Renaissance Poets*, in the Viking Portable Library series:

> It is nonsense to say that the men of the Middle Ages did not observe nature, or cared only about their own souls, ignoring social relations: indeed it would be truer to say that their intellectual weakness was an oversimple faith in the direct evidence of their senses and the immediate data of consciousness, an oversimplification of the relation between the objective and subjective world. Believing that the individual soul was a microcosm of the universe and that all visible things were signs of spiritual truths, they thought that to demonstrate this, it was enough simply to use one's eyes and one's powers of reflection to perceive analogies. For example:
>
> *As* the soul aspires to God, *so* the stone of the Gothic arch soars.
>
> *As* individuals and armies fight for territory, *so* the virtues and vices struggle for possession of the soul . . . etc.
>
> When Bacon [who alternately spelled his name Bakon, BTW] defines science as putting nature to the question—that is, the torture—he is rebuking this trust in direct observation, for he implies that nature is secretive and must be compelled against her will to reveal the truth. Modern science begins when, instead

of asking what a thing is like, for which simple observation is enough, one asks how long it is or how heavy, questions which cannot be answered without performing experiments. When the break came it was drastic. Luther denied any intelligible relation between Faith and Works, Machiavelli any intelligible relation between private and public morality, and Descartes any intelligible relation between Matter and Mind. Allegory became impossible as a literary form, and the human Amor seemed no longer a parable of the Divine Love but its blasphemous parody.[20]

It was into this world that WS stepped, and the path he took has never been so fairly seen as in Honan's *Life*—my candidate for the definite biography of our age, in its unassailable and well-shaped assurance.

Yet it is Bloom who exposes the other side, the antipathy under academic interest, which hopes to avoid the personal diminishment that comes from contact with a canonical writer of such clear mastery as WS, in its rush to embrace the fashionably *au courant*—the elevation of theorist over text. When this took place it was a transfer of German "higher criticism"—used to adjudicate the "primitive" and therefore unknowing authors of texts of the Bible—inside the academy's tower.

Many academies want to keep up with Yale and it was Yale in the 1990s that was characterized by Bloom, in his contribution to the *Harper's* cover story examining the plausibility of de Vere and other pretenders to the throne, as "shot to pieces."

OTHER TEXTS TO CONTEMPLATE

Berryman's Shakespeare, by the late *Dream Song* poet, published posthumously,[21] has the textual finickiness one might expect from a person as attentive to rhythms and sounds as Berryman, yet a scholarly admiration even over trifles in *Lear*. Auden's lectures on Shakespeare, delivered off the cuff at the New School in the late 1940s, were also only recently published,[22] and contain perhaps the most partisan and original views on the plays—sparks scattering from one poetic genius rubbing against another. Or all the plays except *Merry Wives of Windsor*. Auden found it so awful he instead played a recording of Verdi's *Falstaff*. Both are books of creators enamored of the Creator. And the creative John Updike, never a laggard in a landslide, entered the lists with his prickly novel, *Gertrude & Claudius*, in which Claudius is Gertrude's first love. Updike is not fan of *Hamlet*, as per his introduction, and has often noted his dislike of rustics and gravediggers, as intellectuals and anti-Stratfordians (he is not one) tend to dislike them.

Two contemporary writers on the subject I would recommend are Ron Rosenbaum and *The Shakespeare Wars*, and the way it leads into another, Stephen Greenblatt's *Will in the World*. Rosenbaum relates some of the high-stakes intellectual issues taking place in scholarly realms, the new ways of looking at WS, and his book, as critics have pointed out, could have been reduced by a hundred pages—*maybe*. Its obsessive nature, its circling return to a mind-altering performance of *Midsummer Night's Dream* in the sixties, is behind its page-turning power, as I suspect an editor realized; it reads like a mystery. One WS war is "the new historicism," as it is known, promoted and partly invented by Stephen Greenblatt: the idea, to simplify, is that the matrix of a local culture of a specific era will squeeze, as it were, the words out of a writer, so whoever that writer might happen to be is of no import. Or that was Greenblatt's view until he wrote a page-turner of his own, *Will in the World*, a biography that seems to assert that the writer is after all the center of an oeuvre, and especially the Will we know as WS.

The depth of the thought of WS is elucidated in *Shakespeare the Thinker*, by A. D. Nutall, a wonderful book, and further carried forward in *Shakespeare's Philosophy* by Colin McCann.

It was of course Dr. Johnson, Enlightenment angel and compiler of the first excellent English dictionary—besides sitting as subject for the most obsessive but enduring biography—who first applied the press of intellect to the intellect of WS in his *Preface* to the plays. Till then WS was considered not much more than a popular and esteemed playwright, one of several in the golden era of British dramaturgy. Early on Johnson says that

> to works not raised upon principles demonstrative and scientific, but appealing wholly to observation and experience, no other test can be applied than length of duration and continuance of esteem.[23]

This, for him, the work of WS clearly claims, and the genius of WS is that

> he found the English stage in a state of the utmost rudeness; no essays either in tragedy or comedy had appeared from which it could be discovered to what degree of delight either one or other might be carried. Neither character nor dialogue were yet understood. Shakespeare may be truly said to have introduced them both amongst us, and in some of his happier scenes to have carried them both to the utmost height.[24]

And it was Johnson who decided that the unities governing Greek tragedy—unity of action taking place over a single period of time in a single place—were absurd. "Whether Shakespeare knew the unities, and rejected them from design, or deviated from them by happy ignorance, it is, I think, impossible to decide, and useless to inquire."[25]

To expect a playwright to observe these unities, when the London playgoer knew he wasn't in Athens but was willing to make the imaginative leap seemed, perhaps, absurd, along with the next logical thought: Why not move to other places, with leaps in time? The only necessary unity in drama, Johnson decided, was action or plot. And about the distinctions between types of plays, Johnson said:

> Shakespeare's plays are not in the rigorous and critical sense either tragedies or comedies, but compositions of a distinct kind; exhibiting the real state of sublunary nature, which partakes of good and evil, joy and sorrow, mingled with endless variety of proportion and innumerable modes of combination; and expressing the course of the world.[26]

As per Bloom. With his sonorous intellect, Johnson pried at the corpus and opened a few of the floodgates that the best critics over the centuries have been parsing into tributaries since. The news, if it need be named, is that the outpouring of words and thoughts from the work of WS is inexhaustible. What are the qualities that make it so? Why does its center hold, cohere, and lead more generations of followers up the many tributaries toward its source, an enigma so overwhelming no amount of commentary seems to define it?

RUMORS AND CONCLUSIONS OF AN ACTOR'S LORE

The psychiatrist Gerald G. May notes in the first sentence of *Addiction and Grace*, "After twenty years of listening to the yearnings of people's hearts, I am convinced that all human beings have an inborn desire for God. Whether we are consciously religious or not, this desire is our deepest longing and most precious treasure."[27]

That longing and treasure, once reached, gives an adherent's inner (if not outer) edges a weight of glory and meaning in what may otherwise seem humdrum everyday existence, however an adherent may define the road to faith. After forty years of reading WS and acting in roles in which I had to memorize pages of his poetry, I came to believe that he, more than any writer in my native tongue, bears an inborn gravitation to God. The will or quest to know God as fully, through others, as WS is able to do, is the enigma that possesses us as we follow the actions his words portray to a play's completion.

A further side to who he was and what he wrote is found in the preface to an edition of his *Complete Works* by a nineteenth-century British actor, Sir Henry Irving, who states, "When the Baconians can show that Ben Jonson was either a fool or a knave, or that the whole world of players and playwrights at the time was in a conspiracy to palm off on the ages the most astounding cheat in history, they will be worthy of serious attention."[28]

WS died, and Jonson composed an ode whose somewhat grudging opening suggests, along with "would he had blotted more,"

Jonson's green-eyed envy over WS, but as he continues its eighty lines he commemorates WS as a man of quality and a playwright—the poem first prefacing a book of 1623, *William Shakespeare: Comedies, Histories, and Tragedies*, the first folio, as it is known, the first printed collection of WS plays, thirty-five of them compiled by the two heroes already mentioned, Hemmings and Condell.

Down a dozen lines in his ode, Jonson, a classicist, enters the memorializing that this genre of poetry is meant to convey:

> I, therefore will begin. Soule of the Age!
> The applause! delight! the wonder of our Stage!
> My *Shakespeare*, rise; I will not lodge thee by
> Chaucer, or *Spenser*, or bid *Beaumont** lye
> A little further, to make thee a roome:
> Thou art a Moniment, without a tombe,
> And art alive still, while thy Booke doth live,
> And we have wits to read, and praise to give.[29]

Later, when Jonson died and notebooks he kept came to the fore, his own hand records how a person named Shaksper kept interfering with his advance. The playwright Webster, a later contemporary, refers to the "copious industry" of the person he knew as "Shakespeare," besides Robert Greene's "upstart crow, beautified by our feathers," who had the audacity to see himself as "the only Shakes-scene in the country," the pun itself suggesting a country boy, not to say a specific name—this before his plays received any sort of popular acclaim in London.

If the man was so great, why weren't tomes written about him while he lived, or soon after he died? Why aren't they written about America's greatest fictionist, a nearer contemporary to us, Herman Melville? In Melville's case, other than his own books and letters to Hawthorne, he was relatively taciturn and the earlier part of his life was spent at sea.

Besides this, in Elizabethan England, an actor's position was so low in laddered society it fell at the approximate level of a prosti-

---

*These three are buried in Westminster Cathedral, Shakespeare under the floor of the Stratford Church.

tute. The person was an untrustworthy practitioner of scurrilous half-magic that could not be called art, if the practice wasn't downright seditious. Jonson was hauled to court on a homicide charge, for killing an actor in a sword fight, a duel, and was released not because the charge was not valid but because he held a divinity degree from Oxford and could plead "benefit of clergy," meaning that he could read and write and so wasn't, one has to assume, an ignorant murderer. He was, however, branded at the base of his thumb with a T, which meant death on the gallows at Tyburn for any further capital offense.

The rebellion of the Earl of Essex was claimed to have been given added heat by a viewing of *Richard II*, and the Lord Chamberlain forbade WS's company to stage the play for a while, as court and other available history records. Kit Marlowe, the only contender to the artistry of WS, suggested in his plays the possibilities spoken poetry could take, but before he reached his maturity he was stabbed in a pub brawl, a poniard entering an eye socket, according to the autopsy. Such was the practice of theater.

Its seamy reputation in the seventeenth century is the reason players and playwrights and not the court or the academy took up the cause of WS, once dead. Who else dared, given that no one knew how royalty would react? After Bloody Mary and shilly-shallying Elizabeth (who had Mary Queen of Scots and others beheaded, however, along her indecisive route) and then the braying fop who took the throne and felt compelled, it seems, to prove via the theology of the Scots Presbyterians he hated, as only English schoolboys hate a master, that he was equal to the Pope. He set himself as superior to British prelates and scholars on the theology of witchcraft, and declared his intent to publish a new Bible. His interest in it waned, and the translation was unhindered by his royal touch—*The King James* (or *Authorized*) *Version*, as it is called to this day. WS appears to have had no hand in it, although that rumor is another that has circulated at various times.

It wasn't until Victoria, three hundred years down the line, that

Henry Irving brought enough panache to the office that he became the first tragedian, the first actor ever in British history (up to then), to be knighted, in 1895. About the transition at the end of Victoria's reign, Tony Rennell, a biographer, the author of *Last Days of Glory,* of Victoria, says, "In this world and this society, distinctions of class and money meant so much. They defined every aspect of life. On the surface, they were as unyielding as the weather."[30]

Imagine those strictures three centuries before. WS was a good enough guy, considering the business he was in, but an outcast, not only as an actor but also a Stratford bumpkin, familiar with tanning and leather and sheep and wheat and woods and pasture, now residing in the New York (New York of our era, with Paris combined) of his time. He was perhaps allowed to lead a horse of the lady of a manor to a hitching post, as legend has him at his first job, but a lord or duke or wealthy merchant would attend more to his own shadow than to a stable boy. Farmers and rural folk were below that—mere peasants.

But WS was an astute businessman and manager, and that is what has made him stick, much as artistes may dislike that; two of the acting companies he was part of enjoyed the royal prerogative, employed by two separate courts; and two incarnations of the Globe Theatre prospered. Through all of this he built up investments in his place of birth, Stratford. He saw to it, probably at a price, that his father, John, was granted a coat of arms; he bought New Place in Stratford in 1597, a commodious manor of ten rooms, "much as it was in the poet's youth (Honan),"[31] and his wife Ann was able to move their three children from his father's house. WS is listed by the Queen's Council as one of the hoarders of malted barley (meaning sprouted and dried, providing a high sugar content for brewing) in Stratford in 1598, all those eighty bushels; and in the only extant handwritten letter to WS, two Stratford aldermen beg him for a loan. He made good money.

Sharers in his acting company "were earning about £1 a week (probably the equivalent of £500 or more in London at the end of the twentieth century). This was four times the fixed wage of a skilled city worker, and his income would have been between £100 and £160 a year from all sources" or in present-day American terms about $160,000 to $180,000 a year.[32]

Ben Jonson, playwright and poet and deviser of court masques, who, like Herrick, also composed songs ("Drink to me only with thine eyes") was never quite able, along with every other writer of the time, to depict the wider world and its spectrum of human-kind with the inclusive embrace of WS. Jonson was a classicist and a theologian, with a tendency toward ballroom wit, as with his remark of how WS should have blotted more, and the under-current of interplay between Jonson and WS is set in light by the Irish writer Frank O'Connor, when he compares Faulkner's lack of European panache or education to O'Connor's fellow Irishman, James Joyce, in *Writers at Work, The Paris Review Interviews, First Series*:

> [Faulkner] really is ingenuous. Joyce was not ingenuous. Joyce was a university man. *Paris Review*'s interview with Faulkner reminded me strongly of the description that Robert Greene gives of Shakespeare. All the university men of Shakespeare's day thought he was a simpleton, a bit of an idiot. He hadn't been educated, he just didn't know how to write. And I can see Faulkner approaching Joyce in exactly the way that Shakespeare approached Ben Jonson. Look at the way he imitates Ben Jonson in *Twelfth Night*—just a typical Jonson play—doing the best he can to be like Jonson and all he succeeds in doing is to be brittle. I'm really thinking of the time he came under Ben Jonson's influence—that would have been about the time *Julius Caesar* was produced. Jonson has a crack somewhere or other about Shakespeare's being so uneducated he didn't know Bohemia didn't have a seacoast, and he mentions how he used to talk to the players about the horrible errors in Shakespeare's plays. He quotes from *Julius Caesar*— "Caesar doth never wrong, but with just cause"—and he says, "I told the players this was an absurd line." Shakespeare [or an editor] cut it out of *Julius Caesar*, it's no longer there.[33]

A FINAL FUGAL QUEST

The meaning of his tragedies, and most of the comedies, too, is made plain to any in the audience by the base, simplistic, even often off-color scenes that include the antics of clowns, rustics, and unfettered spirits of fun. This was the route WS continually took, an irritant to those who want him to be a stoic classicist. Louise Bogan pictures him properly in a quatrain entitled "To an Artist, to Take Heart":

> Slipping in blood, by his own hand, through pride,
> Hamlet, Othello, Coriolanus fall.
> Upon his bed, however, Shakespeare died,
> Having endured them all.[34]

The master-maker, in the deathbed serenity Bogan suggests, was able to endure the onslaughts on his personality and conscience and consciousness that the production of his characters—the release of them! the outpouring of them!—must have caused, and this is the overarching nature of his accomplishment. The smile in so many of his portraits assumes the lines of "Mona Lisa," a da Vinci self-portrait, as X-ray tomography has revealed—a retreating gaze in a face like a mask, so that WS as *person* becomes our focus of interest.

He continues to ignite electricity along our edges from his assured residence within the immortality he best describes for himself, in the sonnets especially—see *Shakespeare as Literary Dramatist*, by Lukas Erne, or the strange story of his likeness in Stephanie Nolen's *Shakespeare's Face*.

He understood his characters from the inside and liked to mimic them (through characters in low-comedy scenes) and knew how to enact them; few ring false notes, as actors affirm. He had an affinity and affection for all of his characters, every one. Yet in many ways, as an artisan, he is as distanced from them as from the people he brushed past each day on the London streets, those we never hear about and so was *somewhat* detached, poking fun at one aspect or another of a character in a few lines, consistently hitting a sort of sore comic hot spot.

It is this precision of focus that underscores all great tragedy, as WS must have seen from the first, perhaps while he copied out a Latin poem in grammar school or, better, as most schoolboys were required to do in good schools up to the time of Randall Jarrell and W. H. Auden, translated a poem from Latin into his own verse. And as a country boy schooled in Virgil and Ovid, he was attuned to the pastoral world.

He delivered gloves for his father and one of his trips likely took him to the Hathaways, a well-set-up family at Shottery, beyond the place where, today, soccer fields border the edge of Stratford and woods begin. If we try to enter the woods of WS in the way he entered his characters, an apt analogue might be entering his characters as Old Testament writers viewed Elohim—the plural majesty of a single God. Writers in English sooner or later have to acknowledge that anything estimable they achieve has its origins in Shakespeare, considering his efforts to straighten and broaden a language that included multitudes of foreign overtones and accents; his addition of over ten thousand words to its vocabulary—his unabashed double entendres centuries before Freud, the ease of mastery over the simplest yet most complex phrase, especially in the era after *Hamlet*, the play in which he unloaded most of whatever in him remained unresolved in a rat pack of words, and then moved on.

In his native isolation and affinity for the actual, the original, the primitive, he is the best linguistic guide to the English language, and we step nearer to who he was by his words and their rhythms and the multitude of characters he fitted together as messengers of his many permutations. Through his characters, in a further way, he speaks to us as an *integrated bearer of ultimate Good News*. Above all, he placed the impress of Christ, whose outlines are love and mercy and reconciliation, into more universally appealing characters than any other writer in the history of the Western world.

He was in the main a writer of *feeling*. The symphonic interchange of emotion between every variation of class and gender in his work, but especially between men and women, are mouthfuls of magnificent poetry—an achievement readers and auditors of the plays continue to wonder at. We read him in the twenty-first century to discern the depths of those relationships in ways that others are unwilling or unable to describe. Freud's grasp of the inner workings of gender specificity, for instance, was a vague undercurrent to the sea available in WS.

He was an actor by trade and a wanderer, in his life and his imagination, setting his plays across a global landscape. And he was a bard, one who has to keep the range of variations a speaker is able to orate under control. He admired Latin poets for their georgics and agrarian acumen (he was no slouch, with expertise gained in actual work with animals and the land), plus the oddities of love and its transformations in Ovid. He sympathized with the Greeks' insight into the tragedy of an existence with no outlet, no hope, no exit, and had an affinity for any who viewed life in those terms, as Marlowe, his contemporary, did. Other writers of the era glimpsed the predicament (moderns identify it as existential), but WS faced it head-on, with a pacific smile of patience behind his variety of guises.

His view of the potentialities of an exit, first in furtive glimpses and then fully, considering the reconciliation the characters in his later romances achieve, allows us to live in hope and leads us to acknowledge him as the master of human nature.

Few before or since have sensed the intersection of one's words on a page with immortality quite as he did, and his sonnets and plays can be viewed as variations on enacting immortality.

People and the situations they work themselves into (always of attraction and repulsion) revolved through his mind as the planets of a galaxy revolve around its sun. He had a nearly perfect trust in the natural turning of the world as an internal turning that he must have perceived, considering his creative process, as the center of a separate universe. Stars revolve in orderly perpetuation through their seasons as kings and queens and princes and clowns and fools appear and disappear and then reappear again in an endless pageant that stormed through his mind and senses. He watched with the grave and liturgical attention of a spaniel, and then reconstructed actions as songs and translated into words the dreamlike cast of the visions and fantasies of those he observed in the most relaxed and textured containers of measured verse one can find in English.

As the worldwide culture becomes more "global," in the popular parlance (which means more than a McDonald's everywhere), it is relearning as a culture the wisdom of WS and its application to internal and external affairs—his solid sense of consanguinity (a word he uses, meaning *of the same blood*) with the best and the worst in us.

Lore and court records have him returning home at least once a year, and it's likely he went back to check on the lamb crop each spring (along with perhaps cattle, maybe swine) and to oversee the seeding of his barley and wheat, and he would want to be present in late summer or early fall for harvest. He seems to have known from the start that Stratford (farming populace and handcraft merchants) was the source of his accomplishments, and he paid it homage, dying in New House only blocks from where he was born, leaving a healthy largesse to Stratford's poor. Only a person who was nurtured by and nurtured the earth over its diurnal and seasonal changes could have written his plays—rural boy that he was, farmer or farming-inclined son of a rural tradesman and farmer.

The older, unmarried Hathaway daughter had a way about her that caught his shopkeeper-herdsman's eye, a sharp-tongued beauty, Beatrice to his bony Benedict of eighteen. She was enough older it might have seemed all but heresy to conjoin with her, an unhappy but arousing reminder of the accessibility yet forbidden consanguinity of one's mother, as seen in Mosaic Law (a "primal, eldest curse"), now a common malady, the Oedipal oogenesis of mystical mother love.

She was certainly not an old maid, as a number of thoughtless commentators have pegged her, and here Honan comes to her rescue with the statistic that the common age of marriage for women in that area of England, in that era, was between twenty-four and twenty-six. And an entire case in point is made for Anne by Germaine Greer in *Shakespeare's Wife*. Well, then, in the unquenchable courage of youth, WS talked to the older woman—she was twenty-six—perhaps as he lay at her feet beside the Avon (a courtly country swain if not yet a courtier), head propped on a hand propped by his elbow, and perhaps only intimated that they might try a nonmarital yet marital relation before they were betrothed, just once—Shakespeare in love; the *try* and *just once* gaining leverage—and when she turned up pregnant and they married (both from churchgoing families, with WS's father perhaps in the midst of a quandary over the Catholic Church, as recent evidence suggests), marriage was for them for life.

She, the older, wiser woman, should have known better, and couldn't quite forgive him; she told him so and didn't care whether he moved out; she let him know her mind, as Beatrice did, and would endure what she must with his black spot of tuppery shadowing her.

In *Winter's Tale*, one gets a sense of how he gained forgiveness: let her thaw from his separation (and perhaps defensive accusations) and begin anew. She added verbal fire to his feminine edge, and by the time she started asking him to spend time away from the house, now that her female organs were ruined by the birth of twins (still living with his parents), he had every scene with her set in his mind on his first long walk to London—two to three days on foot.

The best and worst of the advances in metaphysics and science and Western philosophies and religions were present in London, besides a polyglot language of the kind we encounter in Chaucer, with foreign accents and overtones of meanings undermining every other word, so that Defoe, a century later, still referred to it as "your Roman-Saxon-Danish-Norman-English"—the residents of Europe's grand city aware of Machiavelli's *The Prince*—that scary treatise on political power that memorialized their fears of royalty. Most of them were opposed to Roman Catholicism as the true church, at least in public, as Sir Walter Raleigh's and Bacon's thoughts were imbibed, but especially in this metropolitan center of a prodigy of a country that was incorporating several languages into its vocabulary, in the midst of managing the spelling and pronunciation and general onrush of it; printing coming into its own, moving from the purview of the church to cut-rate booths encircling St. Paul's, the center of the city—all this present, plus "the little Latin and less Greek" that a rural schoolboy would know, each day a shifting storm of separate cultures you had to name in their manifestations and separate parts, only to find your words melted away by the next morning.

WS appears in the glimpses that remain to have enjoyed the city, the work, and the camaraderie, not only with his players but with Jonson, Marlowe, Alleyne, and Kyd spurring him on. He sensed that music was language made pure, musical language alone worthy of the ultimate communion, love, so that "If music be the food of love, play on!"

The society he observed was composed of the strata of classes that persist in present-day England. The fenced-off fortress of the privileged, the bastion of upper class, forbade communication with those a rung below (this is what Jane Austen's novels, to appear a century later, are about), much less the hayseed no-account who might lead to you the horse you had a servant saddle, all the way down to a household factotum. WS and a few of the backwoods bumpkins he depicted were barely of the class to hold a horse's bridle. No lord or aristocrat would dare imagine or put down on expensive paper such dunderheaded dolts as Dogberry and Verges.

The most violent of his lovers' spats, from *The Taming of the Shrew* to *Winter's Tale*, were sweetened at the end by reconciliation, and the way he reconciled himself to London, to its artistic and cultural ambiance and aristocracy, while separated from his wife and family, is yet another mystery. But a compressed sonnet, dating from early in his career, before success fully struck, offers clues:

When in disgrace with fortune and men's eyes,
I all alone beweep my outcast state,
And trouble deaf heaven with my bootless cries,
And look upon myself and curse my fate,
Wishing me like to one more rich in hope,
Featured like him, like him with friends possessed,
Desiring this man's art and that man's scope,
With what I most enjoy contented least;
Yet in these thoughts myself almost despising,
Haply I think on thee, and then my state,
Like to the lark at break of day arising
From sullen earth, sings hymns at heaven's gate;
    For thy sweet love remembered such wealth brings
    That then I scorn to change my state with kings.

This sweet love is surely Anne's. He saw to the care of her and their children financially, and bought her the second largest house in Stratford, so they could move from his parents' place. He was a nurturer, as Anne likely was, and tended to his land and animals and garden, as other sonnets and plays reveal, recording the labor and details of these activities with authority. On his walks in rural Stratford he observed flowers and crops and wildlife with the eye of an ecologist; it is doubtful you will find in any contemporary so many varieties of plants given voice in their seasonal differences and profusion. What he saw once he preserved in the unassailable ether of his mind.

He viewed himself as disunited, gathering blackberries when he would rather hunt a buck; from the beginning viewing himself as filled with such pinpoints and fissures and interstices of little meaning (except for the light they shed on one or another of the characters he released)—or anyway saw himself as no better than any he mocked and so entered their tableaux and served at the foot of kings, a durable, dependable Stratford lad. The internal equipoise he appears to have achieved served as a source he was able to call upon when, at the unexpected arrival of a cataclysm of words, he tried again to reinvent himself as integrated and whole, the Many in the One.

About the Essays

"Guns & Peace," originally titled "Guns," first appeared in *Esquire*, December, 1975; was included in *Mom, the Flag, & Apple Pie: A Bicentennial Salute*, ed. staff of *Esquire*, Doubleday, New York, 1976, and has been anthologized, in whole or in part, in *The Sense of the Seventies*, ed. Dolan & Quinn, Oxford University Press, New York, 1978; *Forms of the Essay*, ed. Milan & Ruttson, Harcourt, Brace, Jovanovich, New York, 1979; *Prose Models*, 5th Ed., ed. Gerald Levin, Harcourt, Brace, New York, 1981; *The Random House Reader*, ed. Frederick Crews, Random House, New York, 1981; *Strategies in Prose*, ed. Farrell & Salerno; Holt, Rinehart & Winston, New York, 1983; *The Writer's Voice*, ed. Sandra Loy, Holt, Rinehart & Winston, New York, 1985; *Before and After: The Shape and Shaping of Prose*, ed. Emblem and Solkov, Random House, 1986; and *Prose Models*, ed. Gerald Lynch, Gerald Levin & David Rampton, HBJ-Holt Canada, 1993.

"Homeplace, Heaven or Hell?" was first given as a talk at the Conference on Christianity and Literature at Northwestern College, Orange City, Iowa, Spring, 1983; was presented in part, with additions, at "Looking Ahead to Home," sponsored by *Image* and the Graduate Theological Union, Berkeley, California, November, 1992; was published in a recast, expanded format in *Renascence*, Vol. 44, No. 1, 1991; and here includes updated content.

"Views of Wendell Berry," appeared in the *Washington Post Book World*, January 31, 1981, under their title, and reappeared in an expanded, recollected version in *North Dakota History*, Vol. 49, No. 3, Summer, 1982, and since has been updated to include more current Berry publications.

"AmLit," under the title, "Resurrected Light," appeared in *Books & Culture*, September-October, 1995.

"Gardner's Memorial in Real Time," titled "Mickelsson's Ghosts," first appeared in the *Chicago Tribune Book World*, June 13, 1982; in an expanded version, "Mickelsson's Ghosts: Gardner's Memorial in Real Time," in *MSS*, Vol. 4, Nos. 1 & 2, Fall, 1984, and has been revised and slightly enlarged with updated afterthoughts.

"Gospels of Reynolds Price," titled "The Word Made Fresh" (my title), appeared in the *Washington Post Book World*, May 5, 1996, and here takes an expanded and revised cast.

"Updike's Sheltered Self," originally appeared in *The World and I*, December, 1992, and an expanded version, divided into sections, was being serialized in *The Bias Report*, from winter into spring, 1995, just as that publication closed down; I have included obvious additions since.

"Deconstructing God," originally titled "Teaching the Fourth 'R'," appeared in *Civilization: The Magazine of the Library of Congress*, May-June, 1995, and has been updated to include recent publications.

"Dylan to CNN," appeared in *Image: A Journal of the Arts and Religion*, No. 28, Fall 2000, and was reprinted in *Bearing the Mystery: Twenty Years of Image*, ed. Gregory Wolfe, Wm. B. Eerdmans, 2009, and appears here with updated additions.

"The Faith of Shakespeare," originally appeared in *Books & Culture*, September-Octtober 2004, and here has been revised, shifted into subject divisions, and expanded to include Shakespeare publications, productions, and ephemera that have surfaced since.

NOTES

CHAPTER 2: HOMEPLACE, HEAVEN OR HELL?

1. Georges Bernanos, *Essais et écrits de combat I* (Paris: Gallimard, 1971).

2. William Blake, "The Clod and the Pebble," in "Songs of Experience," in *Blake's Poetry and Designs*, eds. Mary Lynn Johnson and John E. Grant (New York: Norton, 1979), 42.

3. See Theodore Roethke, *Selected Poems* (New York: Library of America, 2005), especially the poems from *The Lost Son: And Other Poems* (1948).

4. William Blake, *The Notebook of William Blake: A Photographic and Typographic Facsimile*, ed. David V. Erdman (Oxford: Clarendon, 1973), N92 transcript, MS 5.

5. John Updike, "Home," in *Pigeon Feathers and Other Stories* (New York: Knopf, 1962), 168.

6. Allen Bloom, *The Closing of the American Mind: How Higher Education Has Failed Democracy and Impoverished the Souls of Today's Students* (New York: Simon and Schuster, 1987), 25.

7. Graham Greene, *Collected Essays* (New York: Viking, 1969), 115.

8. Ibid., 115–16.

9. Wendell Berry, *Recollected Essays: 1965–1980* (San Francisco: North Point, 1981), 306.

10. Ibid., 306–7.

11. Ibid., 308.

12. Ibid., 309.

CHAPTER 3: VIEWS OF WENDELL BERRY

1. Wendell Berry, *Recollected Essays: 1965–1980* (San Francisco: North Point, 1981).

2. Wendell Berry, *What Are People For? Essays* (New York: North Point, 1990), 9.

3. Wendell Berry, *Sex, Economy, Freedom & Community: Eight Essays* (New York: Pantheon, 1993), 173.

4. Berry, *Recollected Essays*, 151–266.

5. From "A Native Hill," in ibid., 108.

6. Ibid., 110.

7. "Christianity and the Survival of Creation," in Wendell Berry, *The Art of the Commonplace: The Agrarian Essays of Wendell Berry*, ed. Norman Wirzba (Berkeley, CA: Counterpoint, 2002), 305–20.

8. Wendell Berry, *A Part* (San Francisco: North Point, 1980), 15.

9. "The Mad Farmer March," in ibid., 347.

10. "Discipline and Hope" in Berry, *Recollected Essays*, 155.

11. Ibid., 188.

12. Ibid., 219.

13. "Body and Earth" in ibid., 315.

CHAPTER 4: AMLIT

1. John Gardner, *On Writers and Writing*, ed. Stewart O'Nan (Reading, MA: Addison-Wesley, 1995).

2. Ibid., vii.

3. John Gardner, *The Art of Fiction: Notes on Craft for Young Writers* (New York: Random, Knopf, 1984), 87.

4. Gardner, *On Writers*, 35–36.

5. Ibid., 75.

6. Ibid., 140.

7. Ibid., 174.

8. Ibid., 73–74.

9. Ibid., 166.

10. Ibid., 167.

11. Ibid.

12. Ibid., 168.

13. Ibid.

14. Ibid., 169.

15. Ibid., 170.

16. Ibid.

17. Ibid., 171.

18. Ibid., 123.

CHAPTER 5: GARDNER'S MEMORIAL IN REAL TIME

1. Vladimir Nabokov, *Lectures on Russian Literature*, ed. Fredson Bowers (New York: Harcourt Brace Jovanovich, 1981), 141–42.

2. Ibid., 142.

3. John Gardner, *Mickelsson's Ghosts: A Novel* (New York: Knopf, 1982).

4. Ibid., 7.

5. Thomas McGuane, *Panama* (New York: Farrar, Strauss and Giroux, 1978), 95.

6. Erick H. Erikson, *Gandhi's Truth: On the Origins of Militant Nonviolence* (New York: Norton, 1969), 180.

7. Gardner, *Mickelsson's Ghosts*, 4.

8. Ibid.

9. Ibid., 7–8.

10. Ibid., 4.

11. Ibid., 5.

12. Ibid.

13. Ibid., 11.

14. Ibid., 31.

15. Ibid., 16.

16. Ibid., 9.

17. Ibid., 17.

18. Ibid., 33.

19. Ibid., 25.

20. Ibid., 40.

21. Ibid., 63.

22. Ibid., 29.

23. Ibid., 78.

24. Ibid., 239.

25. Ibid.

26. See ibid., 129, 481.

27. Ibid., 136.

28. Ibid., 329.

29. Ibid., 215.

30. Ibid., 419.

31. Ibid., 76.

32. Ibid., 560.

33. Ibid., 578.

34. Ibid., 590.

CHAPTER 6: GOSPELS OF REYNOLDS PRICE

1. Reynolds Price, *Three Gospels* (New York: Scribner, 1996).

2. Ibid., 234.

3. Ibid., 18.

4. Michael Robbins, "Beauty's Not Generous: Four New Books," *Poetry*, December 2008, 277.

5. Price, *Three Gospels*, 22.

6. Ibid., 17.

7. Ibid., 87.

8. Ibid., 134.

CHAPTER 7: UPDIKE'S SHELTERED SELF

1. Peter Buitenhuis, "The Mowing of a Meadow," *New York Times Book Review*, November 14, 1965, BR4.

2. John Updike, *Of The Farm* (New York: Knopf, 1965), 58–59.

3. Norman Mailer, "Some Children of the Goddess: Further Evaluations of the Talent in the Room," *Esquire*, July 1966.

4. John Updike, *Hugging the Shore: Essays and Criticism* (New York: Knopf, 1983), 851.

5. William Maxwell, interview by John Seabrook, "William Maxwell, The Art of Fiction No.71," *Paris Review* 85 (Fall 1982), http://www.the parisreview.org/interviews.

6. Updike, *Of The Farm*, 107.

7. Ibid.

8. Updike, *Hugging the Shore*, 877.

9. Updike, *Of The Farm*, 153.

10. Ibid., 151.

11. John Updike, "Earthworm," *Collected Poems, 1953–1993* (New York: Knopf, 1995), 29.

12. Updike, *Of The Farm*, 59.

13. John Updike, *Couples* (New York: Knopf, 1968).

14. John Updike, interview by Charles Thomas Samuels, "John Updike, The Art of Fiction No. 43," *Paris Review* 45 (Winter 1968), http://www.the parisreview.org/interviews.

15. Ibid.

16. Marilynne Robinson, "Puritans and Prigs," in *The Death of Adam: Essays on Modern Thought* (New York: Macmillan, 2005), 152.

17. John Calvin, Preface to *Olivétan's New Testament* (1535/43), in Calvin's Commentaries, ed. and trans. J. Haroutunian; LCC 23; (Philadelphia: Westminster, 1958), 70.

18. Robinson, "Puritans and Prigs," 169.

19. Alexander McCall Smith, "Lost in Fiction," *Wall Street Journal*, April 4, 2009, http://online.wsj.com/article/SB123880307592488761.html.

20. John Gardner, *On Writers and Writing*, ed. Stewart O'Nan (Reading, MA: Addison-Wesley, 1995), 171.

21. Updike "Seven Stanzas at Easter," *Collected Poems,* 20.

22. John Updike, *Marry Me: A Romance* (New York: Knopf, 1976), 287.

23. John Updike, "Leaves," *The Early Stories, 1953–1975* (New York: Random House, 2004), 513.

24. Updike, *Couples*, 96.

25. Updike, *Marry Me*, 145.

26. John Updike, "Still Life" in *Pigeon Feathers and Other Stories* (New York: Crest, 1982), 27.

27. John Updike, *Self-Consciousness: Memoirs* (New York: Knopf, 1989).

28. Ibid., 41.

29. Ibid., 34.

30. Ibid.

31. Ibid.

32. Ibid., 35.

33. Ibid., 32.

34. Updike, "Flight," *Early Stories*, 52.

35. Updike, *Self-Consciousness*, 80.

36. Ibid., 102.

37. Ibid., 103–4.

38. Updike, "Minority Report," *Collected Poems*, 102.

39. Updike, *Self-Consciousness*, 31.

40. John Updike, *Rabbit, Run* (New York: Ballantine, 1996), 5.

41. Updike, *Self-Consciousness*, 35.

42. Updike, *Rabbit, Run*, 5.

43. Updike, *Self-Consciousness*, 41.

44. John Updike, interview by Charles Thomas Samuels, "John Updike, The Art of Fiction No. 43," *Paris Review* 45 (Winter 1968), http://www.theparisreview.org/interviews.

45. Updike, *Self-Consciousness*, 33.

46. Ibid.

47. Ibid., 232.

48. Ibid.

49. Updike, "Seven Stanzas at Easter," *Collected Poems,* 20.

50. John Irving, *A Prayer for Owen Meany: A Novel* (New York: Random House, 2002), 3.

51. Updike, *Of The Farm*, quoting Jean-Paul Sartre [see *Essays in Existentialism* (New York: Citadel, 1993), 58].

52. Updike, *Self-Consciousness*, 123.

53. Ibid., 230–31.

CHAPTER 8: DECONSTRUCTING GOD

1. Stephen L. Carter, *The Culture of Disbelief: How American Law and Politics Trivialize Religious Devotion* (New York: BasicBooks, 1993), 35–36.

2. Ibid., 36.

3. Ibid.

4. Ibid., 38.

5. Martin Luther King Jr., "Letter from Birmingham City Jail," quoted in ibid.

6. Warren A. Nord, *Religion and American Education: Rethinking a National Dilemma* (Chapel Hill, NC: University of North Carolina Press, 1995).

7. Ibid., 39.

8. Ibid.

9. Ibid., 47.

10. Gerald Graff, *Professing Literature* (Chicago: University of Chicago Press, 1987), 85, quoted in Nord, *Religion and American Education*, 83.

11. Nord, *Religion and American Education*, 96.

12. Ibid., 131.

13. Ibid., 123.

14. Anthony Bryk, Valerie Lee, and Peter Holland, *Catholic Schools and the Common Good* (Cambridge, MA: Harvard University Press, 1995), 302.

15. J. Gresham Machen, *Education, Christianity, and the State*, ed. John W. Robbins (Jefferson, MD: Trinity Foundation, 1987), 100.

16. Ibid., 102.

17. Ibid., 100.

18. Ibid., 101.

19. Ibid.

20. Ibid., 112.

21. Ibid.

22. Ibid., 147.

23. Ibid., 149. Quoting from Kenneth Strike, "Review of Five Home Economics Texts," unpublished ms., 52.

24. Jonathan Franzen, "Good Neighbors," *New Yorker*, June 8/15, 2009, 78–89.

25. Nord, *Religion and American Education*, 242.

26. Ibid., 181.

27. Ibid., 232, *Gallup Poll: Public Opinion 1986* (Wilmington, DE: Scholarly Resources, 1987), 243.

28. Ibid., 360.

29. Ibid., 149.

30. Ibid., 150.

31. R. J. Rushdoony, *The Messianic Character of American Education: Studies in the History of the Philosophy of Education* (Nutley, NJ: Craig, 1963), 322, quote from "Parochial and Public," *New Republic*, March 20, 1961, 4.

CHAPTER 9: DYLAN TO CNN

1. Bob Dylan, "Knockin' on Heaven's Door," *Lyrics, 1962–2001* (New York: Simon & Schuster, 2004), 313.

2. Dylan, "When the Ship Comes In," *Lyrics*, 94.

3. Dylan, "Ballad of a Thin Man," *Lyrics*, 174–76.

4. Dylan, "Rainy Day Women #12 & 35," *Lyrics*, 191.

5. Dylan, "Don't Think Twice, It's All Right," *Lyrics*, 61.

6. Dylan, "Saved," *Lyrics*, 425.

CHAPTER 10: THE FAITH OF SHAKESPEARE

1. Anthony Lane, "Onward and Upward with the Arts: Tights! Camera! Action!" *New Yorker*, November 25, 1996, 65–77.

2. "Looking for Shakespeare," *Atlantic Monthly*, October 1991, 43ff.

3. "The Ghost of Shakespeare," *Harper's Magazine*, April 1999, 35–62.

4. David Mamet, *Three Uses of the Knife: On the Nature and Purpose of Drama* (New York: Columbia University Press, 1998), 13–14.

5. Robert Greene, *Greene's Groatsworth of Wit: Bought with a Million of Repentance* 1592; repr., Binghamton, NY: Center for Medieval and Early Renaissance, State University of New York at Binghamton, 1994).

6. Robert Frost, interview by Richard Poirier, "Robert Frost, The Art of Poetry No. 2," *Paris Review* 24 (Summer-Fall 1960), http://www.theparis review.org/interviews.

7. Ibid.

8. Charles H. Shattuck, *Shakespeare on the American Stage, Vol. 2: From Booth and Barrett to Sothern and Marlowe* (Washington, DC: The Folger Shakespeare Library, 1987), 309.

9. "The Ghost of Shakespeare," *Harper's Magazine*, April 1999, 35–62.

10. Harold Bloom, *Shakespeare: The Invention of the Human* (New York: Riverhead/Penguin Putnam, 1998), 402.

11. Ibid., 383–431.

12. George H. Morrison, *Christ in Shakespeare: Ten Addresses on Moral and Spiritual Elements in Some of the Greater Plays* (London: J. Clarke, 1928), 7.

13. Ibid.

14. Ibid.

15. Ibid., 72–73.

16. Ibid., 73.

17. The majority of these are from Sir Henry Irving's prefatory essay in William Shakespeare, *The Complete Works of William Shakespeare* (New York: P. F. Collier, 1900).

18. Park Honan, *Shakespeare: A Life* (Oxford: Oxford University Press, 1998), xiv.

19. See, for example, S. Schoenbaum, *William Shakespeare: A Documentary Life* (New York: Oxford University Press, 1975).

20. W. H. Auden and Norman Holmes Pearson, eds., *Medieval and Renaissance Poets: Langland to Spenser* (New York: Viking, 1950), introduction.

21. John Berryman, *Berryman's Shakespeare*, ed. John Haffenden (New York: Farrar, Straus and Giroux, 1999).

22. W. H. Auden, introduction to *William Shakespeare: A Documentary Life*, edited by W. H. Auden and Norman Holmes Pearson (New York: Viking, 1950).

23. Samuel Johnson, *Preface to Shakespeare*, Project Gutenberg, ebook No. 5429 http://www.gutenberg.org/ebooks/5429.

24. Ibid.

25. Ibid.

26. Ibid.

27. Gerald G. May, *Addiction and Grace* (San Francisco: Harper & Row, 1988), 1.

28. Shakespeare, *Complete Works*, xliii.

29. Ben Johnson, "To the Memory of My Beloved the Author, Mr. William Shakespeare."

30. Tony Rennell, *Last Days of Glory: The Death of Queen Victoria* (New York: St. Martin's, 2000), 60.

31. Honan, *Shakespeare*, 31.

32. Ibid., 225.

33. Frank O'Connor, interview by Anthony Whittier, "The Art of Fiction No. 19," *Paris Review* 17 (Autumn-Winter 1957), http://www.theparis review.org/interviews.

34. Louise Bogan, "To an Artist, to Take Heart," in *The Blue Estuaries: Poems 1923–1968* (New York: Ecco, 1977), 104.

Coming in September 2011 *from* **Larry Woiwode**

"One reads Woiwode as much for the power and stunning beauty of his prose as for any story he chooses to tell...."

The Philadelphia Inquirer

"Mr. Woiwode has a poet's sensibility, and his scenes can resonate with perfect descriptions, not a detail astray."

The New York Times Book Review